Praise for the]

"... In its understanding (and forgiveness) of human selfishness and weakness, and in its encouragement always to seek the good. *Secrets* is a profoundly humane book. I wept when I read it...I also laughed aloud - more than I cried. In the many anecdotes and lessons I recognized my own worst fears and flaws, and for once felt willing to forgive myself my own shortcomings and try again, instead of feeling guity and giving up...It is a book that I will return to repeatedly. I have already recommended it to friends in one life crisis or another; I think *Secrets* would help them stop berating themselves over everything that is not right with their lives and go about making what is good better."

-- Anita Buck
Tanglewood Editorial

"Chan has managed to tell a story on one level, with a message on another and made it poetic on yet another level. ...*Secrets* deals firmly with fundamentals of life and martial arts according to Chinese precepts, yet in a way westerners can understand. It bridges a gap that no other similar book has done."

--Kent Mitchell
The Atlanta Journal Staff Writer

"In its simplicity, the story unravels the complexity of the inner working of the human mind...a great therapeutic book for its readers."

- Sunny Lu, Ph.D., M.D.

"...images from the book have continued to resonate in my mind long after I've finished reading it; surely it will touch others deeply, too. ...The book is full of wisdom: basic truths that the world is so very much in need of learning, or remembering. In the fable-like narrative, *Secrets* points the way to realignment with cosmic truth. It's almost as if Lao Tzu had written a novel! A treasure in a lacquer box. Thank you for writing it."

--Beth Franks
Editor and author

"It is a wonderful book with many uplifting qualities. Chan did a fine job of bringing traditional stories and poems and lessons together into a cohesive whole. ...I liked the combination of the fanciful with the sensible. In fact, yin and yang are well-balanced throughout this book: It is informative but not preachy, erudite but not stuffy, humorous but not silly. The work is like the proverbial needle in cotton, the strength of the lessons wrapped in the softness of the story. There is much to be learned and much to be enjoyed throughout the progression of the story. Above all, it is readable. The characters are engaging, and the plot is simple yet interesting. It was delightful."

--Pat Rice
Director of "A Taste of China" Taijiquan

SECRETS
OF THE
TAI CHI CIRCLE:
JOURNEY
TO
ENLIGHTENMENT

Luke Chan

BENEFACTOR
PRESS

A Special Dedication:

This book is dedicated to my aunt, Wai Lim Chan, and my late father, Koon Sing Chan.

My aunt held my family together during its most vulnerable years when four children were growing up without a mother. Without her unselfish love and strict supervision, my life would have taken another course and this book would never have been written. From the depth of my heart, I say, "Dear Aunt, thank you. Your efforts have not been in vain."

My father's belief in my education was uncompromising. There was a time when he was sick and food was hard to find. I pleaded with him to let me quit school and find a job to support myself. He stood there like a rock, unmoved by my pleadings. A lesser father would have taken the easy way out and released his son into the work force prematurely, but mine didn't. I meant to say this when he was alive, but now he has gone. Anyway, here it is, "Father, this book is for you. I love you."

Acknowledgements:

Throughout the entire book, I have lavishly borrowed ideas from the ancient Chinese scholars, poets, philosophers, and religious leaders. I am greatly indebted to them.

Practicing and getting the benefits of Tai Chi for twenty-five years, I am grateful to all my Tai Chi teachers for their generous teachings and inspiration. Among others, Master Tu Chung-king and Master Wang Pei-sheng.

I would like to thank those people who have helped me, encouraged me, and given me suggestions on my book. They are: Master Zeng Wei-qi, Beth Franks(who also helped edit), Kent Mitchell, Anita Buck, Barbara Pratt, Pat Rice, Benson Wu, Warren Ha, Martha Kang, Bob Gepfort, Dr. Xu Tingsen, Robert Allen, my Tai Chi students, and others.

I would like to make special mention of my father-in-law, Lu Jian-hua, for his stories have inspired me; and my mother-in-law, Hu Yi-sun, for her hospitality while I was in China researching this book.

I would also like to thank my brother, Frank Chan, for his honesty in pointing out flaws in my stories and in giving me valuable suggestions.

I want to give special thanks to an inspirational friend, Johnny Chin. Johnny had not only given me suggestions on the subject of selling and human relationships, but he also exemplified how it was done in the course of conducting his business and dealing with people. My life has been enriched because of this friend.

After I had finished my first draft of the manuscript, it took me a year and a half to revise and rewrite it. So during this long period of waiting, who did I call when I need some editing? Dr. Henry Felson. Who did I call when doubt crept into my mind? Dr. Henry Felson. Who has read my manuscript over and over again and never gotten tired of it? Dr. Henry Felson. I am very fortunate to have this gentleman as my friend and mentor.

Finally, I want to thank my wife for her ideas and insights, not to mention her patience with my erratic creative behavior--I sometimes stayed up until dawn or sometimes sprang up from the bed during the wee hours to catch a few "inspirations." Indeed, my journey of intellectual awakening began when I married her. Maybe I have not given her enough credit most of the time, for I am a proud man. Yet this book could easily have been co-written with my wife, Sunny.

Contents

Chapter One

Lotus

"My dear son," said my mother as she handed me an ancient lacquer box. "Today you have turned eighteen and I now turn over to you a great family treasure. For more than eight hundred years our family has passed down this special box from generation to generation. You may open it." When I opened the box, I found a broken jade plate inside.

My mother continued, "My dear son, this precious plate was fashioned by one of our ancestors, who, during his time, was a great scholar as well as a great general. This sage had developed a martial art as a way of life and taught it to the members of the royal family. Unfortunately, he was slandered by jealous competitors in the Imperial Court, and lost his favor with the Emperor. He fled to the south and changed his identity to avoid prosecution. Before leaving his family, he broke this jade plate in two and gave one half to his beloved wife, telling her that like the plate, his heart was broken, and hoping that one day they would be united again. He also told her that the plate itself was a secret pathway to enlightenment, but that to receive its illumination, his sons must learn about it directly from him, or in case of his death, from the disciple in possession of the other half of the plate. And that whenever their oldest son should come of age, she should give him the broken plate and encourage him to seek his father.

"Father and son died without locating each other. But the idea of finding the person in possession of the other half of the jade plate, so that we could profit from its wisdom, has inspired our family for generations. Since you have become an adult today, you are now responsible for the safekeeping of this family treasure." My mother took the jade plate out of the lacquer box and placed it in my hands.

As I touched the broken plate, a strange feeling came over me. Instead of asking myself why I should carry on such a long and probably fruitless tradition, I asked myself, how could I possibly find the other half of the jade plate?

"Mother, do you remember teaching me this poem:
Your son has the desire to go beyond this village.
If I study not to be a success I will never return;
I need not be buried in this Mulberry field when I die.
Where is there a green mountain I cannot be?"

My mother nodded and I continued, "I have always wanted to travel and learn from the outside world. But I have never gotten up enough courage to ask your permission. Now when I touch this plate, Fate calls out loudly for me to go. Mother, may I have your blessing to leave?"

Tears flowed down my mother's cheeks for she had lost her husband and now her only son wanted to go away. Quickly she wiped away her tears and said softly, "My son, I know I cannot keep you here forever. Follow your dreams wherever they may lead you. But my dear son, when the spring grass turns green next year, will you be back then?" I knelt down before my mother and promised her that I would come home soon.

Next morning I bade my mother goodbye and embarked on my journey to discover the secrets of the jade plate.

Where can I begin to look for the other half of the plate? I asked myself. I reasoned that since my ancestor had invented a martial art form, he must have taught it to some students. In turn, his students would have taught it to others, and if the art had been beneficial to people, it should still be practiced today. So I decided to study martial arts taught by famous teachers wherever I would find them, hoping that they could help me in my search.

I studied conscientiously with a number of teachers and learned all that I could from them, but when I showed them my plate, none were acquainted with it. I soon exhausted all the famous martial art teachers in the area and finally decided to leave the province.

On my way southward, I passed through a marketplace where I saw a muscular youth bullying an old man. He had taken a bunch of ginseng roots from the old man and started to walk away without paying. When the old man tried to stop him, he threw a fist toward the old man's chest, but he missed. He tried again to hit the old man from another angle, and again missed. The youth became extremely angry and vandalized the old man's selling booth, scattering the goods everywhere.

When the youth began to kick the old man, I could bear it no longer and stepped in just in time to ward off the attack. The young bully, surprised by my intervention, immediately faced me in fighting position. I surveyed my opponent and saw I was in for a rough fight because he appeared to be strong and quick. But I had learned well from my masters and was confident enough to fight him at close range. I finally defeated him and he limped away.

I was exhausted and sat down on the curbstone to rest. By this time the old man had gathered his ginseng and came over to thank me. He examined my bruises, assured me that I was not seriously injured, and advised me to leave at once to avoid further fighting. But it was already too late as the young bully had come back with his teacher.

"Who was the nasty man who broke my student's nose?" the teacher shouted.

The old man bowed to the teacher and said, "Master, big men have big hearts; please let bygones be bygones. I apologize for what has happened to your student."

"This is between the two of us," said the teacher, pointing at me and ignoring the old man.

There were a thousand voices telling me to fly rather than fight, since I was tired and my body was aching. A stronger voice commanded me to stay, saying, don't leave this old man unprotected! Don't disgrace your family name! I made up my mind instantly that I would not dishonor myself by walking away. So it was settled that I would fight.

But I was no match for this teacher; he was as strong as a horse, with biceps twice as large as mine. The teacher wasted no time in hitting me squarely on my nose, breaking it.

"Please master, now that you have avenged your student's broken nose, please make peace," begged the old man.

The teacher gave the old man a hostile look and continued to hit me so violently that I was forced onto a nearby bench. I knew I had done all I could, and now only a miracle could save me from my deadly enemy. Seeing my predicament, the teacher raised his foot, jumped high into the air, and was about to deal me a finishing blow. As I sat helplessly looking at his gigantic foot coming down, down, down, suddenly I felt a small force, which was just enough and just in time to pull me out of the way and save me from the killing foot. The foot landed on the bench and broke it into two pieces!

When I recovered from the surprise of my sudden good fortune, I realized that the old man had come to my rescue. He was now fighting the teacher. As I watched, the teacher slid a quick step forward and threw a punch toward the old man's head. The old man seemed to have read his mind, for in a flash he raised his right hand to meet the attacking arm halfway. The old man's hand stuck to his opponent's arm as if glued to it. Like a sparrow caught in a net, the teacher struggled to free himself from the hand; and when he tried to use force to disentangle himself from the trap, the old man made use of this force and threw him at least ten feet away. The teacher knew he was defeated and quickly walked away with his student.

"Thank you, sir. You have saved my life," I greeted the old man.

He smiled and said, "My child, indeed, I need to thank you for your courage in trying to protect me."

"I am sorry I couldn't do better, sir. But I am glad that I have found a good teacher today. Will you teach me your martial art?" I asked.

"I should be delighted to have you as my student since you have shown me your courage and kindness today. But there is a family oath which forbids us to teach persons outside our own family. Besides, the fight is not over yet," the old man replied.

"What do you mean, the fight is not over yet? I saw it with my own eyes. Have you not clearly defeated the teacher?" I asked in surprise.

"Yes, but he, too, has a teacher," he replied.

The old man was right because soon the teacher came back with his master. I was surprised to see that each higher ranking master had a bigger and stronger body than his student. This man was as big as a buffalo, with "a tiger back and a bear waist." When he walked, I could almost feel the earth shake!

"So who was the guilty one?" asked the master sarcastically, looking at the two of us. When the old man stepped out, the master was surprised, for he had thought it was I.

"Don't joke with me, old man. If you try to protect your son, you, yourself will be in trouble," he warned.

The old man spoke calmly, "He is not my son, young master, and it is I whom you are looking for. This fight was started by your student who tried to steal my ginseng. Now I want to make peace with you, young master. Please let big things become small and small things become nothing. Let's go our separate ways."

But the master would not listen. He took off his outer garment to expose his biceps and his muscular body. Then he stared at the old man to see if this showing of force had any effect on him.

"However, if you want to fight, I will fight you," the old man continued, ignoring the show of strength.

The master, seeing that this old man was not impressed with his muscles, signaled his student to give him a wooden board. He raised his bare hand and broke the board into two pieces, accompanying this activity with a terrible yell.

The old man picked up the two broken pieces of wood and put them on the curb as if he were cleaning up the debris and not himself involved in the fight. The old man's strange behavior puzzled the master. Why did he take the show of force so indifferently? Wasn't he the one who had defeated one of his best students? This master, who had years of street fighting experience, did not view this old man lightly. With great concentration, he put up his fists and was ready to attack. However, when he found that the old man had deliberately left his body wide open and unprotected, he was baffled. For a moment, he hesitated to attack because he was wondering how the old man could defend himself with his guard down unless he was playing some sort of trick.

Suddenly the old man put his hand into his pocket and shook it purposefully, creating a metallic sound. Thinking the objects inside the old man's clothes could be secret weapons, the master and his students fled.

Once they were gone, I immediately addressed the old man, "Let's go, sir. They might come back."

"No, my child, they won't be back," replied the old man.

"How can you be so sure, sir?"

"My child, when the young bully tried to steal my ginseng, you defeated him. When the young bully's teacher came and defeated you, I defeated the teacher. Then came the teacher's master, trying to defeat me. As you see, my child, violence begets violence, and it never ends. Of course, finally the master defeated himself and the chain of violence ended."

"Was he defeated?" I asked. "I did not see any punches being exchanged."

"Indeed, my child, we did fight, but we fought with our minds. The master tried to create fear in my mind by demonstrating the power of his body. I neutralized his attack by ignoring his show of force. Then I attacked him by creating doubts in his mind, deliberately opening up my body for him to attack. When I made some metallic sound using coins in my pockets, his doubts turned into fear. Finally his fear convinced him to leave. When he reaches his school, he probably will tell his students that he left because he did not want to hurt an old man. So the fight has ended without further injuries."

I became interested and asked, "Sir, if the master had actually fought you, could you have defended yourself?"

He smiled and answered, "Does it make any difference? It is all in one's mind, my child."

I was fascinated by this old man, for he seemed to know more than just martial arts. I asked again to be his student.

"There is the family oath that I must not break." After saying this, he disappeared into the crowd on the street.

Family! Family oath! Family tradition! How much are they worth? I was a bit discouraged. But isn't it family loyalty that has allowed our civilization to survive more than four thousand years? I comforted myself. Then I realized that I should follow this old man since he might change his mind, but he was nowhere to be found. I went back to where he had sold his ginseng and saw another vendor there. "Who is that old man who was here just a few minutes ago?" I asked. The vendor replied, "Everybody calls him Grandmaster. Seventy years old. Looks like sixty, doesn't he?" "Yes he does. Can you tell me where he lives?" "At the famous Chen Village, thirty miles from here." "What is the Chen Village famous for?" "Tai Chi Chuan, of course. Most people call it Tai Chi for short." "What is Tai Chi?" "Nobody knows except members of the Chen family. Some say it is a kind of martial art and some say it is a way of life. All the people from Chen's family are very nice, and they are happy people. However, they have never taught Tai Chi to anyone outside their family circle. In fact, my family has been living next to the Chen Village for centuries and we are still trying to learn the art from them!" He shook his head in despair.

After finding the directions to the Chen Village, I embarked at once and reached the village just before sunset. Grandmaster was delighted to see me, put me up in his guest room, and asked me to stay a few days in order to heal my bruises. I again asked him to teach me Tai Chi, but he politely declined.

Next morning I was awakened by the songs of birds. Looking through the window, I saw Grandmaster exercising. His movements were effortless and graceful, as if he were dancing among the clouds. Sometimes he stood up on one leg and extended his hands just like a white crane courting; sometimes he crept like a snake dancing in the springtime; and sometimes he moved his hands dexterously like a virtuoso playing lute.

Then when he raised his right hand in a circular motion, I immediately recognized the same movement he had used to defeat the young teacher! Indeed, Grandmaster was practicing Tai Chi! As I paid closer attention to his movements, I discovered that the gentleness of his body had tremendous strength within, like needles wrapped in cotton; all his movements followed circular paths, and like a sphere, he could easily ward off attacks from all sides. Even though I could distinguish each offensive and defensive movement, I could not discover where any one movement began or ended. Like water flowing continuously in a mountain stream, the movements were without beginning or end.

After he finished the Tai Chi form, Grandmaster took a sparrow from a birdcage and put it on one hand while his other hand was gently brushing the sparrow's tail. Whenever the sparrow tried to fly away, Grandmaster relaxed his hand just enough so the bird had no solid ground to take off from! On discovering I was watching, Grandmaster put the bird back into its cage and pretended he was merely feeding it. I asked him to teach me but again he kindly refused. I continued to ask him each day, but the answer was always no.

It was time for me to go, as I had completely healed my body. After giving thanks to Grandmaster, I mounted my horse and started my journey southward. I rode along a mountain trail abounding with wildflowers. The flowers made the air so sweet that I couldn't resist taking deep breaths of this fresh mountain air, filling my body with energy. I moved quickly forward until I reached a wide open area.

The scenery was magnificent and I was delighted to be here. I could see a beautiful pond which had a surface so smooth that it looked almost like a mirror. Beyond the pond were fields of green luxuriant grassland surrounded by pine-covered mountains. I could smell the wonderful scent of the pine needles and could hear birds singing. Just in front of me, two squirrels were jumping and chasing each other. Everything existed in peace. "It is a place of great harmony!" I exclaimed as I dismounted from my horse.

Then I realized I was standing underneath a huge tree in an old graveyard. Suddenly I saw someone move in front of an old grave. It was a woman wearing a white spring dress, kneeling down in front of a gravestone, praying. She had long black hair neatly combed into the shape of a lute and a beautiful red flower in her hair.

While I was looking at her there was a loud animal cry in the distance. She turned in my direction and our eyes met. For a moment I was mesmerized. I had never seen such a beautiful girl. She had an oval face and a pair of brown sparkling eyes; she had a sumptuous

She turned in my direction and our eyes met. For a moment I was mesmerized. I had never seen such a beautiful girl.

mouth and a body filled with grace and beauty!

Beautiful she might be, but how could I get to know her? If I lost this chance to meet her, I feared that I would lose my chance forever. For some reason I thought that she might be thinking the same thing too. Fortunately I remembered a popular romantic poem in which a lady met a gentleman. Deliberately I recited the poem loud enough for her to hear:

"May I ask where do you live, Sir?
Maiden lives in the north side of the lake.
I stopped my boat to ask you this question.
Perchance we are from the same hometown."
"My home is near the Nine Rivers, Madame.
To and fro I travel through these waters;
We are both residents of the same province.
Yet we didn't know each other until now."

When I finished, she turned around and giggled, "We do not live by the rivers. We live by the mountains."

"We too. I am sorry if I am intrusive. But what's your name?"

"Lotus."

Abashed, she turned back and pretended to put some flowers on the grave. "What are you doing here, Lotus?" As I spoke, I moved toward her. Paying no attention to the ground, I walked into a ditch covered with tall grass and tumbled. The bag I was carrying was thrown to the ground and opened, scattering my belongings everywhere. I got up obviously embarrassed but immediately remembered to look for my broken jade plate. I was relieved when I picked the plate up and found it still intact. Then I realized Lotus was staring at the plate as if transfixed.

Suddenly she said, "Please, you must wait for me," and dashed into the woods. After a while I heard some footsteps approaching and Lotus showed up with Grandmaster himself!

"Grandpa, this is the man I was talking about." Lotus pointed toward me.

"Grandmaster, I...I...I didn't know..." I wanted to apologize because Grandmaster might think I was taking advantage of Lotus. Before I could finish my sentence, he asked me to show him my plate. I carefully placed the plate in his hands. His eyes opened wide! He returned the plate to me and slowly unloaded an object from his bag. I could not believe my eyes! It was the other half of the plate! When we put the broken jade plates together they fitted perfectly! I noticed that the completed jade plate had eight pictures engraved into it, but they were all worn and almost indistinguishable.

"Finally, a completed Tai Chi Circle!" Grandmaster held my hands and embraced me warmly. "For more than eight hundred years we have been tending your Ancestor's grave and waiting for one of you to show up to claim it. I was told that your Ancestor came to our village one day to escape prosecution. He was such a kind and gentle person that our ancestors gave him sanctuary despite the danger of being prosecuted themselves. To repay my family's kindness, your Ancestor decided to teach my family the secrets of the Tai Chi Circle. My family had to take an oath that these secrets should not be taught to persons other than those in our family and in his posterity as well. Before he died, he gave this broken jade plate to my family and told them that his son or one of his descendants would be looking for it one day; and if someday a stranger showed up and matched the other half of the plate, we could teach him the secrets of the Tai Chi Circle, for he would be a son of his family. Since then we have been tending his grave for twenty-six generations! Now that you have finally appeared, we can return to you the responsibility of tending your Ancestor's grave. Of course, if you still want to learn Tai Chi, I will teach you."

"Yes! Yes! I want to learn Tai Chi. When can we start?" I shouted excitedly.

"Right here and right now!" Grandmaster replied.

So after a year of searching, I finally found my Grandmaster who began to transmit to me my Ancestor's Secrets of the Tai Chi Circle.

Chapter Two

Waterfall

I began my first Tai Chi lesson under the huge tree facing the perfectly calm pond. I noticed an inscription on one of the stones:

Putee Tree is my root.

Reflecting Pond is my mirror;

Sweep my body and mind daily I must,

To keep them away from the worldly dust.

"From now on you will work diligently until your body can root itself into the ground like this Putee Tree, and your mind can be as calm as this Reflecting Pond," Grandmaster said, pointing to the tree above and the pond beyond. "For centuries, many Tai Chi masters have strengthened their bodies under this tree and have cleared their minds over the pond. The road to enlightenment will be long and hard. You must have faith that one day you will become a true Tai Chi master."

"I have faith and I will work hard, Grandmaster," I promised.

"Good," Grandmaster continued, "The oldest and greatest book about changes in nature is called *I Ching*. The author of *I Ching*, while in his highest degree of meditation, observed that the universe consists of two parts. He called them yin and yang. Yin and yang are opposites in nature, yet they need each other for their very existence. Your Ancestor was a great scholar of *I Ching* and from it he derived the secrets of the Tai Chi Circle."

He drew a circle with a curved line through its center on the adjacent ground and explained, "This is a Tai Chi Circle with one half representing yin and the other half representing yang. Just as in arithmetic one and two can represent one person and two persons, one bird and two birds, one tree and two trees, and so on, yin and yang can represent day and night, hot and cold, male and female, and so on. Just as we can use the concept of one and two to add and subtract, so we can use the concept of yin and yang to observe and understand things in the world."

"Like I am attracted to Lotus, woman and man, yin and yang?" I spoke what was on my mind, though I felt a little bit embarrassed.

"That is correct, my child. By the way, what is your last name?"

"My last name is Yang."

"I see. I will give you a student name: Yee. Do you like that name?"

"Yes, thank you very much, Grandmaster," I answered, believing that the name must have some special meaning. Then I remembered to ask, "Grandmaster, what about the eight faded pictures on the jade plate?"

"They represent the eight secrets of the Tai Chi Circle. Each picture depicts a beautiful natural scene and each is associated with a secret of the Tai Chi Circle. Your Ancestor realized that one can master the eight secrets only after continuous repetition and reiteration of the secrets, once they are revealed to you. He also concluded that since scenic pictures relax and calm one's mind, why not associate pleasant, relaxing pictures with the Tai Chi secrets? Your Ancestor went on to advise us that each of us needs to find our own eight relaxing pictures which we should commit to memory. Each time we review these mental images, we induce within ourselves a sense of peace and tranquility since these images serve as our sanctuaries. During the day, these pictures will remind us of the beautiful things of the world and lift up our spirits. At night, they will calm and relax us into peaceful sleep."

After the lesson, Grandmaster led me back to his house and assigned a permanent room for me to stay in. He told me he would continue to teach me Tai Chi tomorrow morning at the same place.

Next morning I got up before dawn and went to the same spot. There I prepared to impress Grandmaster by rooting myself to the ground with my legs, forming a difficult low Horse Stance. When Grandmaster came, I asked, "Am I rooted to the ground like the Putee Tree, Grandmaster? Am I better than the other students you have? What rank do you give me?" I was anxious to win his approval.

Grandmaster did not say a word, but came over and pushed my chest with a very light force. My body automatically tensed up to resist.

But as soon as I did, the soft force vanished, causing my body to fall forward. When I moved my body back to adjust my balance I felt another soft force on my chest, causing me to flop.

"Now forget your impatient attitude," said Grandmaster as he started today's lesson. "The true purpose of learning Tai Chi is to rejuvenate your life so that you can become a happy person filled with life-force. Like a spring fountain, Tai Chi will vitalize your body; and like a single spark, Tai Chi will ignite the fire of your mind."

"Come on, Grandmaster, what about the martial art of Tai Chi? Aren't you going to teach me the real secrets?" I asked impatiently.

"Patience, Yee, patience. The self-defense aspect of the art is only a by-product of your enlightenment, not the real purpose of your pursuit of the art. Now imagine you are a pine tree standing in the middle of a storm. Relax your body totally and follow the force of the wind. Never resist it."

"That's easy," I commented as I stood still and relaxed completely.

"Are you relaxed now?"

"Yes, I am, Grandmaster."

As he gave me a small push, my body tensed up to repulse it. "No good. You resisted," said Grandmaster, and pushed me again. By this time I had learned to pull away from him. "No good. You did not follow my force," disapproved Grandmaster.

If resisting was not right and drawing away was not right, I figured that the only choice remaining was to follow the force consciously. So I said confidently, "I am ready, Grandmaster. Try me again."

This time, when Grandmaster pushed me, I concentrated on my body, attempting neither to resist nor to leave his hand.

"No good!"

"Why, Grandmaster? I thought I had relaxed completely," I asked, feeling discouraged.

"If you are concentrating on ways to deal with my hand, you are not relaxing enough. Like the pine tree, you should follow the intention of the wind, and not anticipate it. And just as the pine tree and the wind become one when the wind blows through the tree, so you and I should become one when my hand reaches you; only then can you use my force as if it were your own. Now try again."

I tried and tried but still did not succeed. Instead of becoming disappointed, Grandmaster seemed to become more enthusiastic each time we tried. I, however, started to lose confidence in my ability to learn.

"I guess I don't have the talent to develop this kind of sensibility."

"People do possess such talent and so do you," said Grandmaster.

"I am sure many people have such a talent, but unfortunately I myself lack it," I replied, looking at the ground.

"Why do you say that?"

"Because all my life, people have been telling me that I don't have talent to do this or that. When I want to join their games, they always say they are too complicated for me, and push me aside," I answered.

"So you believe in their words?"

"Well...well...I do," I admitted.

"You are not alone, Yee." Grandmaster patted my back as we sat down next to each other on the grass. "Once there was an old weaver lady who was known for her calmness in dealing with problems. One day while she was weaving cloth, someone told her that her son had been killed by a tiger, but she did not believe the story and continued to weave because she had seen her son not too long ago and there was no tiger in the area where they lived. When another person told her the same thing, she still remained calm and continued to weave. But when a third person came to tell her the same thing, she panicked and went out to search for her son. The mother was greatly relieved when she found that her son was alive and well and that the person who was killed had the same name as her son's and had lived in the mountains.

"You see, Yee, it takes only three persons saying the same thing to convince a calm and intelligent person to believe in something. Yet it happens to us everyday, Yee."

"Grandmaster, were they all lying when they told me that I lacked talent to do this or that?" I asked, feeling I had been victimized.

"No, Yee. In most cases they did not lie, for they, too, believed that they themselves lacked talent to do this or that. Indeed, there are two types of talents--yin and yang. A dog can swim without learning. This talent comes to it automatically; it is the yang type of talent. On the other hand, a person who has not learned to swim will drown if he falls into the water. However, if a person has a good teacher and a place to swim, he will not only learn to swim but will be a much better swimmer than the dog. This talent is dormant, hidden from a person, and is a yin type of talent. Because yin talents are not easily recognized, most people believe, mistakenly, that they lack them.

"Indeed, we all possess the same kinds of talents, only some of us have developed them and some have not. While some of us become outstanding, all of us can develop a certain level of competency in any job or profession if given a chance. Each of us, like a raw jade stone, could blossom into a beautiful jade flower if given the right stone cutter and environment."

"Grandmaster, is something wrong with me when I sometimes feel inferior and sometimes superior to others?" I took this opportunity to ask about what was bothering me.

"No, it happens to everybody, Yee. There are many human skills and nobody has ever mastered all of them--and no one ever will. So while one is skillful in one area he lacks skills in many other areas. He will naturally feel inferior to others when he is called upon to deal in areas with which he is not familiar. On the other hand, he will feel superior when he knows his subject well.

"Unfortunately, when a person has developed a certain talent, he often uses his superiority to intimidate those who have not developed such a talent; being intimidated, a person will in turn intimidate others in the area of his own expertise. The more insecure a person feels, the more is he apt to intimidate others. Some are so vain about their own skills that they behave as though they were superior to all others, forgetting how they themselves had developed their skills in the first place."

He went on to tell me a story. "A long time ago, there was a skillful archer who boasted he had never missed a target within a hundred walking steps. On one occasion he demonstrated his skill to a crowd of people and hit his target easily. The crowd cheered loudly and asked him to do it again. Just as he proudly raised his bow, an oil vendor commented, 'That was nothing special.'

"The archer felt slighted and asked angrily, 'Can you do it?'

'No,' the oil vendor replied.

'Then why did you dare to scorn my skill?' demanded the archer.

'Sir, I didn't mean to disdain your skill. But I have learned, through years of selling oil, that if one does a thing over again and again, one can master its secret.' After saying that, the vendor took out a coin with a tiny hole in it and put the coin on top of an oil bottle. Then he raised his arm and poured oil into the bottle through the hole. When he had filled the bottle, he took out the coin and showed the crowd that no oil had spilled on it. He turned to the archer and said, 'It, too, is nothing special, for I have done this over and over again for many years.' The archer was speechless and left."

After encouraging me to have confidence in myself, Grandmaster suggested, "Now let's return once more to the lesson on Tai Chi movements. The first thing you need to learn is to relax your body like that of a baby at all times."

As we rose, Grandmaster handed me an egg, "Yee, slowly close your eyes and visualize the calmness of the lake and the gentleness of the mountains in the distance.

"Relax your head and your neck. Then relax your shoulders, arms, and hands. Now pay attention to your body and relax your chest, back, waist, and stomach. Relax and release. And then pay attention to your legs and relax your hips, thighs, feet, and toes.

"Relax, release, and let go. Imagine there are some fragrant flowers underneath your feet and you are breathing deeply to extract their fragrance. The flowers may be redolent of ginger, or of sweet magnolias, or of roses; whatever they may be, their aroma makes you feel very pleasant and relaxed. You are feeling more and more relaxed as you breathe deeper and deeper.

"Let all the tensions in your body go. Release and let go. Let everything go. Release, and let go."

As I relaxed my hands, the egg dropped to the ground. I felt completely relaxed as Grandmaster continued, "Imagine that the top of your head is suspended from above and align your body accordingly.

By centering your body, you can relax your muscles naturally. By relaxing your muscles you are washing away all your tensions. Then you are able to bring life energy to every part of your body. All the stresses which have shortened your life are now dropping to the ground. From now on you are functioning better as a person. You are feeling eternal youth."

Grandmaster told me to open my eyes slowly and gradually. We had finished the lesson for today and he told me to practice the relaxation exercise diligently until I could relax like a baby at all times.

I was very excited and practiced the same exercise daily for weeks. But when Grandmaster continued to take his time, not advancing me more rapidly, I became restless. Since I had observed how he practiced Tai Chi, I decided to learn more on my own.

Trying to imitate Grandmaster's performance with the sparrows, I set up a net one afternoon in an open area and caught many sparrows. I secretly brought them to the Putee Tree and started to practice Tai Chi with them. I wanted to learn to relax my hands so that they would not provide a solid ground from which the sparrows could take off. But it was easier said than done. As soon as I put the birds on my hands, they immediately escaped. Then I learned to tie the feet of the birds to my hands so I could exercise with them again and again! I was pleased with my invention but the birds made noise and caught Grandmaster's attention.

When Grandmaster saw me struggling with the sparrows, he came over. "Yee, how long do you think this pond has existed?" Grandmaster asked as he pointed to the perfectly calm pond in front of us.

"It must be older than my Ancestor's grave, otherwise your family would not have chosen this beautiful place for him," I deduced.

"How long do you think it will remain that way?"

"I am sure it will still be around long after we are gone, Grandmaster."

"I, too, am sure. If it takes centuries for nature to change even a little, why are you in such a hurry?"

"But, Grandmaster, I am not a lake and I will get old and die one day. That is why I must hurry."

"Tell me, Yee, what are you hurrying for?" Grandmaster asked patiently.

"I desire to be the best martial art master in the world," I answered with determination.

"This mountain is high," he pointed to the mountain beyond the pond, "but there is always a higher mountain. If your desire is to be the best master, your efforts will be of no avail. You will become a slave of your own desire because you will never be satisfied with what you have now."

"But Grandmaster, I am nobody now and I must hurry to be somebody soon," I answered eagerly, without knowing I was tensing my body.

"Everything takes time and there is a time for everything. You must plant the seeds before you can reap the fruits. Now relax your shoulders," Grandmaster suggested.

I dropped my shoulders instantly and felt embarrassed, for after all, I did not have a relaxed body: I had tried to run before I could walk!

Grandmaster patted my back and said kindly, "Yee, everybody is somebody in his own right and each of us is a Tai Chi Circle. As a Tai Chi Circle, we are perfect at any time."

"Are you saying that I am perfect now?" I asked incredulously.

"Yes, you are perfect now. We are all perfect now even though the yin and yang which fill our Tai Chi Circles are different. You fill your circle with youth, strong muscles, quickness, innocence, and inexperience; I fill mine with old age, weak muscles, slowness, wisdom, and experience. However, the grass always seems to be greener on the other side of the field. Not being satisfied with their own lives, the young are always in a hurry to live the old men's lives; and the old always lament because they cannot relive the young men's lives. But remember that you can be young only once and so enjoy it; as I know I can be old only once, I am truly enjoying myself."

"Grandmaster, how?"

"I celebrate my existence with joy. Since the most noticeable difference between the living and the dead is breathing, each time when I relax and breathe deeply, I realize I am alive and I am satisfied."

"Excuse me, Grandmaster, old people might be more aware of

their existence since their curtains are drawing near. But I am still young; how can I derive happiness out of my existence?"

Grandmaster picked up a flower bud from the ground, handed it to me and said, "Look at this flower bud, Yee. It could have been a beautiful flower. The bud did not ask to be nipped, yet it happened. Life is very fragile." I stared at the bud and understood that I too, could perish prematurely.

"Would you still desire to be the best martial art master if you were to perish tomorrow?" Grandmaster asked while I was still holding the flower bud.

"I wouldn't have enough time to become one."

"What then would you do if today were your last day on this earth?"

When I fancied that it was my last chance to see this world, I found that everything had become nostalgic. I felt as if I were traveling in an exotic place, seeing things for the first and the last time. I started to wonder: If today were my last day in this wonderful world, would I still have time to search for the perfect moment of my life? If not, shouldn't I start to enjoy life now? If this were my last shining moment on my journey through this life, would I still have time to become a master of all people? If not, can I at least be a master of myself? And since everybody is a Tai Chi Circle, perfect in his own right, why should we envy or intimidate others? No longer controlled by my desire to become an ideal person, I felt this moment, indeed, was the perfect moment of my life.

When I told Grandmaster how I felt, he nodded. Then he asked me to show him the posture of my Horse Stance. I lowered my body to form the Horse Stance and he corrected a minor detail of my posture. I knew what would follow: hours of sweating under the Putee Tree, hard work almost to the point of torture. So before he left, I questioned him, "Grandmaster, if I am so perfect at any moment, why am I working so hard to gain the art of Tai Chi? If I am to be perfect in the future anyway, would it make any difference if I work hard or not?"

"Just as day and night exchange continuously, we, too, are constantly changing from one perfect moment to another. The underlying force directing us from one perfect moment to another is nature. Follow the forces of nature and never resist them." Without further explanation, Grandmaster left.

After hours of almost unbearable training, I finally completed today's lesson. Instead of going to my room as I always did, I went down to the Reflecting Pond, trying to understand what Grandmaster had said to me about the forces of nature. With bare feet, I crossed several mountain streams and noticed the streams were constantly replenishing the pond with fresh water. As I wandered along the shores of the Reflecting Pond, I also noticed that the pond water was flowing down to the low land, replenishing some smaller ponds along the way. Even though each pond remained perfectly calm, its water was actually continuously flowing from one pond to another.

When I came across a small waterfall, the sound of water falling on the rocks captured my attention. In a playful mood, I climbed down the rocks and went inside the waterfall. The water fell down in the shape of a canopy, allowing me to remain dry. Like a curtain of jade, the waterfall appeared to be almost transparent and insulated me from the outside sound of falling water.

As I sat amid the wonders of nature, my eyes followed the individual water drops falling down from the top of the waterfall to the very bottom. As my eyes moved rapidly up and down, a thought flashed through my mind, why does water always go downward?

"Because it follows the forces of nature and never resists them." Grandmaster seemed to have answered my question.

Why do people always want to go upward? I asked myself. The answer came readily: because it is human nature to want to rise above one's present state. A student studies diligently to become a better scholar so that he can earn a better position later in life; parents work hard to provide a better environment for their children; a musician practices day and night to perfect his art. All human endeavors are motivated by people wanting to move upward.

So it became apparent to me that water ponds, though perfect at their present levels, follow nature to course downward to other perfect ponds; whereas people, though perfect at the present moment, follow nature to move upward to other perfect moments of their lives. If a

As I sat amid the wonders of nature, my eyes followed the
individual water drops falling down from the top of the waterfall
to the very bottom. As my eyes moved rapidly up and down, a
thought flashed through my mind, why does water always go
downward?

water pond does not follow the course of nature, it dies, for it remains still and stagnates; likewise, a person who has no aspiration dies, for he vegetates and his mind degenerates.

I came out of the waterfall and found the Reflecting Pond as smooth as a mirror. I became excited as I now understood that working hard toward a higher level of art is a gift to mankind. I raised my hands high and ran along the Reflecting Pond, exhorting myself, "What kind of difficult work can't I do? What kind of obstacles can't I overcome? No, there won't be any because I will tolerate, I will endure, and I will work hard. Oh, yes, I will work harder to reach a higher level of living! I will work harder! I will work harder! I will work harder!"

While I was acting like a hungry giant, never satisfied with what I have, I suddenly realized there was another part of me which was as satisfied and contented as the Reflecting Pond itself. This part of me was asking myself, "Am I not like a water pond, perfect at my present level? If now is my perfect moment, what am I waiting for? Enjoy life now! Enjoy life now! Enjoy life now!"

I understood that yin and yang were coexisting within me to form a perfect Tai Chi Circle: The yang part of me was exhorting me to work harder toward what I wanted in life while the yin part of me was reminding me to enjoy life now.

How do I enjoy life? Then I remembered Grandmaster telling me to celebrate life by being aware I was alive. But how do I know I am alive today? Suddenly a breeze brought the fragrance of honeysuckle to my nose. I followed the scent and found the flowers. Taking a long and deep breath, I smiled and from my heart, I uttered, "Yes, I am alive! Oh, life is such a precious thing!"

As I looked at the Reflecting Pond, I was delighted, for I knew the First Secret of the Tai Chi Circle had been revealed to me. These words repeatedly appeared in my mind, prompting me to live my life fully:

Celebrate life now, for now is my perfect moment; aspire to a higher level of living now, for it is a gift to me.

Celebrate life now, for now is my perfect moment; aspire to a higher level of living now, for it is a gift to me.

Celebrate life now, for now is my perfect moment; aspire to a higher level of living now, for it is a gift to me.

Chapter Three

South Sea

There was a beautiful stream meandering through the Chen Village. Its waters were cool and refreshing as they emerged from the springs of the nearby mountains. I visited this stream quite often because I had discovered that Lotus often went there to wash clothes. One day in order to get her attention, I attempted to stand with one leg on a stone near the water's edge; spreading my hands like a crane ready to fly, I shouted to Lotus, "This is called the White Crane Spreading Wings. Do you think I look like one?" Before she could reply, I slipped and fell into the water!

As I got back to the riverbank, I saw Lotus laughing and heard her saying "You looked more like a Black Turtle Spreading Legs!" Though embarrassed, I was happy to have gotten her attention.

After I had changed my clothes, I went back to see Lotus.

"My grandpa just left for the marketplace; you have already become a lazy worm!" Lotus teased.

"I need a rest, Lotus. Besides, Grandmaster told me to be happy, and I am perfectly happy now!" I raised my hands to the sky to emphasize my point.

"I need to hang up this basket of clothes. If you are not too lazy you may help me," she suggested with a smile.

"My pleasure," I stepped forward playfully and picked up the basket of clothes. Then we headed home together.

We arrived at an open courtyard in the center of the house and started to hang up the clothes on bamboo poles. The courtyard was next to Grandmaster's study, which I had never previously visited. Curious about the room, I looked through the window and saw an old spear and a shield hanging next to each other on the wall. "Those weapons look like antiques. Are they?" I asked Lotus.

"Yes, they are very old and there is a story behind them."

"What is the story, Lotus?"

"Well, you need to ask Grandpa." Lotus signaled me to look behind.

I turned around and found Grandmaster coming toward us. When he arrived, he asked lightheartedly, "Taking a rest, uh?"

"Grandmaster, I am glad to see you. You came back so early today?"

"Yes, the horse cart has broken down again."

"Grandmaster, can you tell me the story behind those weapons?"

"Yes. Indeed, I had intended to tell you the story," he beckoned me to sit next to him. "These weapons were gifts from your Ancestor. One day while walking through a marketplace, he was attracted to a crowd and saw a vendor selling weapons. When customers became interested in his spear, the vendor would tell them his spear was the sharpest one in the world and that it could penetrate any shield. However, when customers became interested in his shield, he told them his shield was the strongest one in the world and could stand against any spear. A customer then asked him, 'Sir, what would happen if I used your spear to strike your shield?' The crowd roared with laughter and called him the Contradictory Vendor. When the Contradictory Vendor tried to explain further, nobody remained to listen except your Ancestor.

"Your Ancestor asked him politely, 'Mr. Vendor, I have heard the same statements made by many other contradictory vendors before. But you seem to be very different from them. Is there something I can learn from you?'

"The vendor replied, 'Since you are a scholar yourself, my customer, you ought to have known that things are made up of yin and yang, and even though they are contradictory toward each other, they still can coexist in harmony.'

'That is very true, Mr. Vendor. Can you tell me more?'

'You see, my customer, the spear and the shield are designed to protect oneself against one's enemies; they become contradictory only when they are used against each other. To the question of which is better, the spear or the shield I cannot give an unqualified answer, for under different conditions, the weapons will behave differently. In a similar fashion, a woman and a man are opposite to each other in many ways but come together to form a family. Who is better, a woman or a man? I cannot answer that question either, for they are different. When a baby encounters a tiger in the forest, the man would probably be better in defending his child; but, when a baby becomes hungry, the woman would be better in providing him with her milk.'

"Your Ancestor thanked the weapon vendor for teaching him an important lesson and bought the spear and the shield from the vendor to remind himself and his followers that contradictory things can coexist in harmony as long as they are not used against one another." Grandmaster finished his story and invited me to his study.

As I entered his room, I immediately noticed a painting hanging in front of his desk. The painting depicted a small bird sleeping peacefully on a bamboo leaf while all other birds were shown sleeping on the ground. A poem accompanied the painting, but I could not understand it. I became curious and asked Grandmaster the meaning of this picture.

As Grandmaster walked toward the painting he said, "I have intended to keep my dream a secret. But I believe fate has brought us together with a purpose and feel I must teach you everything I know. This picture portrays my goal."

"What is your goal, Grandmaster?"

"Pay particular attention to the small bird sleeping peacefully above all the others," he suggested, pointing to the small bird.

I stared at the painting for a long time and then it dawned on me that the bird was resting on a small bamboo leaf! The leaf could not have borne the weight of a feather, yet the entire weight of the bird was resting on it! A small disturbance could easily have upset the balance, causing the bird to fall. The bird and the bamboo had blended into one; only during the highest degree of meditation could this balance have been achieved.

"Grandmaster, can you show me how to set up goals? I want to learn."

"Yes, Yee. The best way to achieve goals is to put them into pictures and words and then persist in pursuing them one day at a time.

Persistence is essential for the achievement of any task. Many people set great goals but do not carry them through because they give up as soon as they encounter obstacles. On the other hand, many people work hard but do not have the wisdom to set goals, and become like oxen toiling in the field. Only a few truly know what they want and work hard toward their goals. There is such a man living in our neighboring village whom many people refer to as the Foolish Old Man. To truly appreciate what goal setting is, you need to visit this interesting man."

I embarked immediately on a visit to the Foolish Old Man. When I reached the village where he lived, I saw a white bearded old man coming toward me carrying two buckets full of soil.

"Sir, I am looking for a gentleman whose nickname is Foolish...Foolish..." I could not finish because calling a person such a name was impolite.

"I am the Foolish Old Man. It is apparent you are coming from afar and are tired. Please come to my cottage and have a cup of tea," he said as he laid aside his buckets and led me to his cottage.

When I entered his cottage I noticed that there was a huge picture conspicuously hung in the middle of the wall. While Mr. Foolish Old Man was pouring tea, I took a closer look at the picture. The mountain depicted in the picture looked exactly the same as the one in front of his cottage, except that in the picture, the mountain was moved to a different position, leaving a fantastic view in front of the cottage.

"Sir, my Grandmaster told me to see you and learn from your wisdom."

He brushed his beard and laughed contentedly, "Everybody in the nearby villages except your Grandmaster laughs at me and calls me Foolish Old Man. They think I am foolish because, as depicted in this picture, I have set as a goal that I will remove this mountain out of my cottage's way. I conceived this idea on the day I retired from working in the field, and I have been removing the mountain ever since."

"Sir, with all due respect, it is a huge mountain and you are..." I said tentatively, cautious not to offend him.

"I am seventy years old, the same age as your Grandmaster. But, look at the houses down the hillside," he pointed to a few specks beyond, "where live my sons and their sons and their sons. The mountain is high but our efforts are endless. When I cannot move on, my son will take my place, his son will take his, whose son will take his, and it will go on endlessly. The mountain might be high but it is still conquerable as long as we persist."

"I drew this picture," he pointed to the picture on the wall, "and deliberately hung it in an obvious place so that I, my son, my son's son, and his son's son would not lose sight of what we are trying to accomplish. A picture is worthy of a thousand words. It keeps our efforts focused and renews our commitment to our goal." He looked at the sun and said, "It is almost noontime. If you would excuse me, I need to continue removing some of the mountain now. Please tell your Grandmaster that I wish him well."

"Before you go, sir, can you tell me how you can keep up with this routine day after day?"

He came closer to me and whispered into my ear as if he were afraid his secret might be overheard, "I have discovered that the most difficult step in completing a journey is the first step. So each day when I go to work, instead of thinking of removing the entire mountain at once, I set a small goal--to remove a tiny part of the mountain only. By doing that I can accomplish my goal one day at a time."

"What if you don't feel like doing anything?" I asked, knowing that he, too, must have had bad days.

"I fool myself," he smiled.

"How?" I became extremely interested.

"When I don't feel like working I set a goal to walk outside my cottage and look at the mountain. By persuading my reluctant body to carry out a seemingly inconsequential goal, I have already taken the first step toward my goal of the day. The next step becomes easier because I have already changed my position from sitting in a chair to standing in front of the mountain. And the next step becomes even easier as I become more active, and soon my body continues to move until I finish my daily work. So long, young man. Remember to persist!"

The mountain is high but our efforts are endless. When I cannot move on, my son will take my place, his son will take his, whose son will take his, and it will go on endlessly. The mountain might be high but it is still conquerable as long as we persist."

I thanked the Foolish Old Man and felt rather excited about setting up high goals. However, on my way home I thought over the lessons Grandmaster had taught me and I became baffled. So I went straight to see him.

"Grandmaster, I am back," I greeted him when I encountered him walking beside the Reflecting Pond.

"Good. What have you learned from our neighbor?"

"He has inspired me to set high goals and persevere in order to achieve them."

"That's good, Yee."

"But Grandmaster, I remember you having told me that if I have a strong desire for a given thing that I will become a slave of that thing. How can I achieve high goals without a strong desire?" I finally blurted out what was bothering me.

"You can if your mind knows how," he replied, seemingly not surprised by my question.

"How, Grandmaster?"

"Tell me, Yee, what goes through your mind when you want to uproot your opponent in the Tai Chi Push Hands exercise?"

"If I am in an Arrow Stance position with my right palm contacting my opponent, I can uproot him by glancing in the direction I intend for him to go, yet at the same instant, my mind is thinking of my right foot and my left palm."

"So you are not obsessed with wanting to uproot your opponent?"

"No, if my mind is preoccupied with winning I will be defeated easily by my opponent. Instead, I am concentrating on obtaining power from the ground and keeping my body in balance: If I hit him, the power will be very great; if I miss him, I will not lose my balance."

"Good, Yee. The same principle applies to setting up goals. Suppose you have set a goal of possessing five horses in one year, and you have drawn a picture of five horses along with a written statement regarding your goal. When you have memorized your goal picture and its statement, the state of yin exists as your goal becomes a reality in your mind; and when you actually take action, the state of yang exists as your action brings it to pass. You will behave as if you had already possessed the horses. Meanwhile, you will concentrate on carrying out the necessary steps to achieve your goal. You will use your mind to find better ways to work and to command your body to work even harder, and you will always be willing to take the extra step to get ahead."

I nodded and asked, "Grandmaster, in other words, my strong desire to possess something is unnecessary because I believe I already possess what I want, and I turn my desire into action?"

"That's right, Yee. If you avoid being obsessed by your desire, you can enjoy and live your life one day at a time while you are working toward what you want. If eventually you have achieved your goal of having five horses, you will not be overjoyed because you knew the feeling of fulfillment ahead of time. Moreover, you will be satisfied with what you have achieved, instead of desiring more horses. On the other hand, if you have not achieved your goal, you will not lose your balance in life because, just as in the Push Hands exercise, you are prepared in case you miss your opponent. So you will not blame yourself for having failed to obtain the horses. Life goes on, and you will not be uprooted emotionally."

"Thank you Grandmaster, I understand now that setting goals is quite a simple process," I said happily.

"Yee, it looks simple, yet it is not. Most people who set up goals believe in paper goals only, not the real thing."

"What do you mean, Grandmaster?"

"Yee, an understanding of what I have just said has to come from yourself. No words can explain it," Grandmaster replied and left.

A moment ago, I thought I had found the key to goal setting, but now I had lost it again. Facing the Reflecting Pond alone, I stood there for a long time. It was a beautiful sunny day with many white clouds floating in the blue sky. The clouds formed interesting shapes resembling different animals--I saw a dog, a lion, and a rooster. The pond was calm and its water reflected the clouds. Birds were flying overhead and horses grazed peacefully in the distant fields. I lay down in the grass, admiring these wonders of nature, and temporarily forgetting my trouble. As I watched the sky, I noticed a few large clouds join to form a huge dragon.

I stood up and stared at the reflection of the dragon in the Reflecting Pond. The dragon reminded me of a story about a painter who was devoted to dragons. The painter thought about dragons all the time and believed in them. He painstakingly painted each dragon with the minutest detail. As a result, he painted a large collection of dragons, all looking alive. Soon his devotion attracted the attention of a real dragon. One day the dragon came to visit the painter to show its appreciation for his belief and devotion. But when the painter saw the real dragon he was horrified and fainted.

As I stared at the dragon in the sky, suddenly, as if the dragon had come alive, it spoke to me, "Do you really believe in dragons?"

"Yes, I do," I replied aloud, thinking about my dreams.

"Then act now on your dreams because what you believe in is real."

"I know I need to turn my dreams into action. But am I ready?" A gust of wind blew the white clouds away and the dragon disappeared before it could answer my question.

I sat and looked at the water in the Reflecting Pond. The serenity of the water had reflected itself in my mind and I became calm. Then I remembered an ancient story about two monks, one poor and one rich. Both monks wanted to make a pilgrimage to the South Sea. The poor monk bade the rich monk farewell as he was about to embark on his journey. The rich monk laughed, "My dear brother, I have been preparing a ship for my pilgrimage for many years. But, you, my brother, what have you done to prepare for your journey?"

The poor monk replied, "My dear brother, I have nothing but a water bottle and a food container." The rich monk laughed loudly and shook his head in disbelief. Without further conversation, the poor monk left for his journey.

When the poor monk returned from his pilgrimage one year later, he found the rich monk was very embarrassed, for he was still preparing his ship.

The story had finally cleared my mind. I ran toward the Reflecting Pond and plunged my head into the cool, crystal clear water. I shook my hair as I came out of the water and jumped high into the sky shouting, "I believe in my dreams, I will act now! I believe in my dreams, I will act now! Act now! Act now!" As I shouted in front of the calm Reflecting Pond, I realized there was another voice within me, advising me urgently, "Use your mind first, plan before you act! Use your mind first, plan before you act! Plan first! Plan first!" Within myself, a Tai Chi Circle was formed--the yin part of me advising me to plan ahead, the yang part telling me to act now.

A big smile spread across to my face, for I had discovered the Second Secret of the Tai Chi Circle. My inner voice was speaking softly and the voice became louder and louder:

Plan for today and resolve to take one step at a time; act now!

Plan for today and resolve to take one step at a time; act now!

Plan for today and resolve to take one step at a time; act now!

Chapter Four

Moonlight

By the time spring turned to summer and summer to autumn, Lotus and I had become good friends. We both loved nature and no matter how the weather turned out, it was always perfect for us. We enjoyed the bright autumn days when the sky was blue and the leaves were red. We also enjoyed the darker days when the autumn rain pattered on the fallen leaves, filling our hearts with romance.

While reading poetry one night when the rain was falling down heavily, Lotus asked me, "Yee, what would you do if we were to be separated?" I smiled as I noticed the poem she was reading:

"You asked me when I will return, I don't know when.

This night the mountain rain has filled the autumn pond;

When can we get together under the candlelight,

And talk about this autumn mountain rain?"

I held her hands for a long time, but before I could gather enough courage to tell her I loved her, she was gone.

Early next morning, Grandmaster and I set out for the mountains to hunt for wild ginseng. Ginseng is a plant which has roots shaped like our human body and is a very effective herb for increasing human vitality. When we arrived at the mountains, the sun was high in the sky and the air had cleared after last night's rain. Indeed, it was perfect weather for hunting ginseng. However, we searched for hours without discovering a single ginseng plant.

When Grandmaster left to look elsewhere, I became bored and started to daydream about Lotus. I dreamt about her beautiful dark hair, her oval face, her charming smile, and her sweet voice until I completely forgot my mission. Suddenly I felt a whack on my head and woke up with a start. It was Grandmaster hitting me with a bundle of ginseng roots. "Yee, it is getting late. Let's take advantage of the sunlight and pick some ginseng."

"But Grandmaster, the sun is setting. Can't we wait until

tomorrow?" I protested.

"Tomorrow, tomorrow, tomorrow, there is always a tomorrow," said Grandmaster, shaking his head. "Let's get to the flowers while they are blossoming, and not wait for them to wither and then harvest empty branches!" He soon disappeared into the mountains, as excited as a child at play. His enthusiasm was contagious: I stood up, took a deep breath and started again to hunt for ginseng.

Ginseng plants grow in hidden places, especially among huge rocks. The more dangerous a place, the more likely ginseng is to grow there. While moving from one part of the mountain to another, I discovered a steep area made up of huge rocks. Determined to find at least one ginseng before the day ended, I started to climb up over the rocks despite the obvious danger. One rock led to another as I clambered higher and higher, not paying any attention to where I was heading. However, when I looked back, I was stunned to see only blue sky beneath me! Realizing I was in the middle of a cliff, I immediately headed back. When I recovered my composure, I looked down carefully alongside my feet and saw a deep gorge underneath me!

Thinking there should be another way off the cliff, I gazed upward. Amid the rocks above me, I saw a beautiful red ginseng flower, as large as a lotus flower, with five crimson petals just barely opened, protruding majestically from the cliff. I now recalled hearing about a rare ginseng plant which had large fragrant flowers instead of tiny clustered bland flowers. Such a ginseng plant seldom bloomed, but when it did, it was known to yield a miraculous substance which could cure all ailments. I was certain that this was indeed the revered flower.

This presented itself as a unique opportunity for me to harvest such a celebrated flower. But even before I made the first move toward it, the thought of failure crept into my mind. For a minute I waited, as my courage and my fear battled each other. However, as neither my courage nor my fear could persuade me to act resolutely, I compromised and started out halfheartedly. But as soon as I started to move, I saw something resembling a snake lying directly in my path! I recoiled and avoided looking up again. Without any further investigation, I assumed that the object I saw must be a snake because it was coiled like one. I further imagined that the head of the snake was triangular, so it was likely to be poisonous! This fearful fantasy convinced me that I should climb down.

But when I took my first step downward, an inner voice stopped me, telling me that I was forfeiting a great opportunity forever. Retracing my step, I closed my eyes and went into my mental sanctuary, breathing in and out slowly and evenly. As I breathed in, I could smell the fragrance of the ginseng flower from above. My mind became calmer and calmer as I breathed in deeper and deeper. Suddenly an image of Lotus appeared in my mind--she appeared ill and was calling my name. Instantly, I knew I had to have this miracle flower, no matter what the cost.

Once I had faith that the flower would be for my dear Lotus, all the walls of fear I had built up in my mind disappeared. When I looked up, the image of the snake had vanished, and I found the "snake" was nothing more than a crooked branch of a nearby shrub!

Focusing on the flower, I moved up cautiously step by step. The flower was hanging in the sky against the brilliant setting sun, filling the air with its fragrance. I tried to reach it with my left hand while my right hand was holding on to the edge of a rock. I could touch the flower but I couldn't grasp it. The flower was so close to me, yet it seemed so far away! I tried and tried, but all in vain. Desperately, I jerked my body to extend the range of my left hand, and reached the flower. I picked the flower, but my feet slipped and I started to fall. In a flash, I remembered my training in Tai Chi: relax, relax, and relax. I released all the tension from my body and became as soft as a newborn child. Like a baby, my body rolled loosely onto the rocky surface and let the fall take its course. When I felt I was no longer falling, I opened my eyes and saw my precious flower, with only four petals left, lying beside me. After putting it securely into my bag, I crawled back to safety.

Reaching the bottom of the very cliff which I had ascended, I saw Grandmaster running toward me. He was very happy to see me safe. Tears came to his eyes when I showed him the flower I had fetched. He took the flower and murmured to himself, "Indeed, the rarest of the rare. They say it can cure all ailments. But what of my loved ones?" I sensed something unusual about his behavior, as if he had some very unpleasant memory about this cliff.

"Grandmaster, why are you crying?" I was anxious to find out.

Grandmaster wiped away his tears and said, "Yee, I am happy that you are alive; but at the same time I feel sad about my son and my daughter-in-law. Ten years ago, my only son tried to fetch a flower from this same cliff, but fell to his death. When his wife tried to save him, she too, perished." Tears poured again from his eyes; he walked away to hide them.

As I thought of the tragedy of Lotus's parents, I now understood why the flower had occupied such a special place in Grandmaster's heart. I carefully put the flower back into my bag and ran toward Grandmaster, trying to comfort him. To my surprise, Grandmaster was already in high spirits, and as enthusiastic as ever--he was now happily counting the ginseng he had gathered today. When I came close to him, I could feel his energy. I had intended to comfort him, but instead I was the one who needed comfort. "Grandmaster, I am still feeling sorry for what happened to your loved ones on this cliff. How can you have switched so quickly from being a sad person to a happy person?"

He smiled and said, "Yee, as human beings, we all have emotions. When we go through life, we encounter many incidents which create strong emotions within us. These emotions come back to haunt us whenever we see cues which bring to mind specific events: The cliff reminds me of the fate of my son and my daughter-in-law every time I see it. Emotions are neither good nor bad, but they are part of our experience traveling through this world. We all want to lead happy lives, enjoying each day as it comes. Since our past emotions tend to limit today's happiness, somehow we must learn to leave them in the yesterday, so we can move on to today and tomorrow. In fact, you have two choices in life, one yin and one yang."

"What are my choices in life, Grandmaster?"

"You either live happily and die; or you live miserably and die," Grandmaster replied.

"I want to live happily, Grandmaster. But how?"

"Yee, let me tell you a story which happened a long time ago. An army led by the Prince of one warring faction was in hot pursuit of his enemies who were trying to join their main force in the North. The Prince's army was now only a few hours away from the point where he planned to intercept his enemies. However, his soldiers were extremely thirsty and could only move slowly because they had been walking in a desert area for hours without water.

"The Prince held an emergency council meeting with his advisors and said, 'My generals, our enemies are not aware that we are intercepting them. If we can reach them before they regroup, it would be our golden opportunity to defeat them. Please tell me what we can do to solve our water shortage problem so that our men can move faster.'

'We can dig some water wells,' one general suggested.

'We have already tried digging deep into the ground in many places. But there was still no water,' answered another one.

'Let us send somebody to fetch water from the wells of nearby villages,' another general suggested.

'I have already sent out some soldiers to find water, but they all returned empty-handed. This is a land with no inhabitants, my dear brother,' answered another general.

'My Lord, I have a bright idea. Can I present it?' a general with a big black beard requested.

'Please proceed, my general,' the Prince replied.

The bearded general signaled to his assistant to bring in a soldier bound with ropes. After his assistant forced the soldier to kneel down before the Prince, the general spoke, 'My Lord, many soldiers complained that they were so thirsty that they could no longer go on marching. I arrested this soldier when I heard him saying we were all going to die of thirst if no water would be found soon. I believe that the best way to keep up the morale of the soldiers is to instill fear into their minds so that they would stop talking about their thirst. Let's use the 'kill one to warn one hundred' strategy by killing this soldier to warn the others, my Lord!'

"The Prince looked at the soldier and asked, 'Soldier, did you say that we were going to die of thirst?'

'Yes, my Lord. It is true. Even if you kill me, there is still no water available for the soldiers. Fear cannot solve the water shortage, for fear, too, has its limits my Lord,' the soldier replied.

'Even if it is true, soldier, you should know that the penalty of spreading bad news in the army is death.'

'My Lord, does it have to be me? Please have mercy on me and let me die in an honorable way fighting my enemies, and not die for telling the truth,' the soldier begged.

"The Prince took a closer look at the poor soldier whose face appeared familiar. 'Haven't I seen you before, soldier?' the Prince inquired.

'Yes, my Lord. I have been a follower of yours through many battles,' replied the soldier.

'If that is so, you must have tiptoed along the line between life and death for many years. Why are you shaking like a leaf now? Are you afraid to lose your life?'

'No, my Lord, I do not fear losing my own life. I fear for the lives of my two young children at home.'

'Why is that, soldier?' asked the Prince in a slightly surprised tone.

'My Lord, if I die in an honorable way for my country, my children would be well cared for by your regime. But who would show sympathy toward the offspring of a condemned soldier? Whenever I think of the story of the Bird Nest, I am fearful about the fate of my children.' The soldier spoke in such a sincere way that his words touched the heart of the Prince.

"The Prince looked into the air and sighed. Indeed, he knew the story of the Bird Nest too well. There was once a general who lost a power struggle with his arch rival. After gaining power, his enemy immediately ordered that the general and his entire family be executed. When the executioner came to arrest the family, the general begged him to free his two children, for they were innocent of any wrongdoing. The children came to their father and embraced him. The younger child of ten said, 'Don't beg, my dear father, we are not afraid. We will go with you.' The older child of eleven raised his fingers and pointed to a bird nest high in a tree branch in their backyard, saying 'My dear father, when the bird nest is destroyed and is turned upside down, can there be unbroken eggs?' Tears came to the father's eyes, for he knew that his children were old enough to understand that their fates were intertwined with his.

"Just as the Prince was about to forgive the soldier and set him free, the bearded general stood up and said, 'My dear Lord, we have run out of options for the water shortage problem. Whether there is one life or three lives at stake, it is a time of war, not a time of forgiveness. Let me kill this soldier and hang his head outside this tent to warn the others.' After finishing his words, he raised his sword, ready to kill the soldier at a nod of the Prince's head.

'Thoughts, not swords. Thoughts, not swords, my Lord,' a voice spoke softly.

"All attention was now focused on the man who had just spoken--the only scholar among all the generals.

'My gentle scholar, why are you so relaxed and even smiling while all of us are so tense over this impossible situation? What have you been thinking, my wise scholar?' the Prince asked.

'Happy thoughts, my Lord, happy thoughts,' replied the scholar.

"There was some soft laughter among the generals as many of them believed that the stress had made this scholar mad.

'Happy thoughts, my happy scholar?' the Prince asked in a curious way and now there was even more laughter among the generals.

'Yes, my Lord. I thought of the moment when I was in love: smiling faces, sunny days, green mountains, blue skies, refreshing water, delicious food, fragrant flowers, just fun, fun, and fun.'

'But my imaginative scholar, those days have already gone by. Like the water flowing downstream, they will never return,' the Prince replied patiently. He did not easily dismiss this scholar as being mad, for the scholar had been sent secretly by the Prince's father, the Emperor, to help him in times of trouble.

'Those moments are always here, my Lord. Right now, as we speak, people are falling in love and celebrating life. In our thoughts, we can join them and celebrate the joy of life.'

'But my joyful scholar, I am the leader of the entire army and all my people are depending on me. They need my experience and intelligence to lead them. I cannot, even in my thoughts, escape to celebrate the joy of life.'

'Why?' asked the scholar.

'If I leave, nobody can replace me. Don't you understand that I am IRREPLACEABLE?' the Prince raised his voice a little.

'Didn't your elder brother say the same thing before he was killed in battle? Since then have you not replaced him and done just as well if not better than your 'invincible' brother? We are all mortals and nobody is irreplaceable, my Lord.'

'I have no more capable brothers to replace me, my scholar. Since the day I took command, I have assumed tremendous responsibility. I have always taken pride in my experience as a soldier and my knowledge as a scholar. I feel I am the only one who can carry the world now.' All the generals nodded their heads in agreement as they listened to their leader speak.

'Yes, my Lord, no doubt you have the strength to carry the entire world on your shoulders,' the scholar agreed. 'But, my Lord, can you put it down?'

'How can I put my world down when I have obligations to my soldiers, my generals, my family, and my Emperor? I have many tasks awaiting me. Only I,' the Prince pointed at himself, 'Only I, have the intelligence and power to do it. For this poor soldier,' he pointed toward the soldier kneeling on the ground and continued, 'Only I have the power to decide his fate!'

'What if you should die tomorrow, my Lord? What happens to your obligations then?' asked the scholar. There was great uneasiness among the generals who felt that the conversation had been carried too far.

'Without fulfilling my obligations, I would die without closing my eyes!' the Prince swore.

'Ropes! Ropes! Ropes!' exclaimed the scholar.

'What ropes, my scholar?' asked the Prince curiously.

'Your obligations, just like the ropes on this unfortunate soldier.

These ropes are holding you while you are alive and they are still with you when you are dead.' This comment prompted some of the generals to put their hands on their sword handles.

"Ignoring the obvious danger, the scholar continued, 'My Lord, being a great scholar yourself, you must understand that things which exist in the state of yang without the accompanying yin are incomplete. If you can carry the world on your shoulders, you surely can put it down, my Lord. When you came into this world, did you bring anything with you? If not, what does this world owe you? When you leave this world, my Lord, can you take anything with you? If not, what do you owe this world? Your obligations exist only in your mind. Those ropes are restricting your freedom, my Lord. Break them! Break them! Break them!'

"Then the scholar spread his hands like the wings of an eagle and continued, 'Free! Free! Free! Free yourself from those ropes and fly high as an eagle. High in the sky, you can see clearly all the possibilities which life has to offer and choose your way of life. If you still choose to carry the world on your shoulders, your burden will no longer be an obligation but a free choice. You will be happy and contented and become a truly successful ruler. Now to solve the problem of water shortage, you will not dismiss the possibility of thoughts.'

'That's absurd!' shouted the bearded general and all others joined him, for they had had enough of this nonsense talk.

'Let him speak!' thundered the prince, for he knew that many brilliant ideas had originated from absurdities.

"The scholar proceeded, 'My Lord, in our thoughts, let's abandon our swords, and--'

'Abandon!' shouted the generals almost simultaneously. They had found the forbidden word they were looking for. They drew their swords out of their sheaths, demanding the head of this scholar. The bearded general pushed the scholar down to the ground next to the condemned soldier. All eyes fixed on the prince, expecting him to order the scholar to be killed on the spot, as otherwise he would face mutiny by his generals.

'Thoughts, not swords, my Lord. Thoughts, not swords, my Lord,'

'Ropes! Ropes! Ropes!' exclaimed the scholar.

'What ropes, my scholar?' asked the Prince curiously.

'Your obligations, just like the ropes on this unfortunate soldier. These ropes are holding you while you are alive and they are still with you when you are dead.'

the scholar repeated calmly. The Prince hesitated for a moment and then beckoned to the scholar to come closer. He listened carefully as the scholar whispered his suggestions.

'Thoughts, thoughts,' the Prince repeated softly as if waking up from a dream. Then he roared with laughter and shouted, 'Indeed, thoughts! Thoughts!' He then ordered the soldier and the scholar to be freed and told his generals to assemble their forces because he had good news for them.

"When the forces were gathered, the Prince spoke, 'My dear soldiers, and my dear generals. Our enemies are within our grasp and we can quickly annihilate them if we can move faster. My vanguards have reported back to me that ahead of us, there are plenty of plum trees full of sour green plums and lemon trees full of green lemons. Just imagine that you have placed an unripe plum into your mouth and bitten into it; the juice of the green plum quickly fills your tongue, your mouth, and your throat; you swallow, swallow, and swallow as much of this extremely bitter juice as you can. After you have finished your plum, you take a large green lemon. Just imagine you have bitten into the lemon and its sour juice immediately fills your teeth, your lips, your tongue, your mouth, and reaches down into your throat. You swallow, swallow, and swallow. Imagine sour lemons, my dear soldiers, sour lemons and bitter plums. There are plenty of sour lemons and bitter plums waiting for us ahead. Let's go and get them.'

"As the soldiers imagined eating the sour fruits, they were temporarily relieved of their thirst and were able to reach their enemies in time and defeated them." Grandmaster finished his story.

"So, happy life, happy thoughts, Grandmaster?" I deduced.

"Yes, happy thoughts, Yee, happy thoughts!"

"But Grandmaster, how can we have happy thoughts when we are expecting to do the very same things over and over on different days?"

"Yee, you need to understand that your mind has two parts. One is the yang part which accepts only what you can see, hear, smell, taste, or touch; the other is the yin part which cannot distinguish fantasies from realities, and acts on everything you believe in. There are many possibilities as to how future events will unfold themselves. Your yang mind will only recognize the most sensible outcomes while your yin mind will recognize any possibilities you may wish to believe. Take our journey home as an example: The most likely possibility is that we will be very tired after a long, monotonous walk. Your yang mind views this possibility as the only sensible outcome, and tells your body so. Having nothing to look forward to but a long and miserable journey, your body will respond by dragging your feet home.

"Though extremely remote, there is another possibility: You are on your way to an exciting place and tomorrow you will be doing something joyful. Your yang mind will automatically reject this idea as absurd. Yet, your yin mind will readily accept it as possible. All you have to do is to believe in this possibility and your mind will do the rest for you, creating a jovial mental environment which will ensure your happiness." Grandmaster stood up and enthusiastically said, "Time to go."

Before I took the first step, I told my yin mind that I was not going to my usual place but to a beautiful place instead. As soon as I began to anticipate my exciting trip, I became energetic and enthusiastic, and the burdens of my routine life disappeared. As I walked, I had a nostalgic feeling about my journey as if I were seeing my surroundings for the last time-- everything seemed so lovely! My steps became so light that I moved like a horse galloping in the springtime.

When we arrived home it was already past midnight. Before going to bed, I put the miracle flower in an underground storage room where the temperature remains constant year-round.

Early next morning I was awakened by a slight tap on my door. I opened the door and found it was Lotus. "I heard you are going to the marketplace today. The weather has become cold so I have been knitting you a sweater," she said softly as she handed me a sweater.

My heart palpitated with excitement and I felt sweet and warm. I donned the sweater and as I was admiring my image in the mirror, I glimpsed Lotus. "What's wrong, Lotus?" alarmed, I noticed that her eyes were red and swollen as if she had cried all night.

"I worried about you and Grandpa last night when you were not back at the usual time. It is dangerous in the mountains," she swallowed her tears as she answered.

"You should know that we will always come back safely. Your worry was unnecessary. Come on, Lotus, you are a grown-up person now. Please, don't behave like a child," I tried to cheer her up, but she ran away, sobbing.

Shocked by her strange behavior, I stood still for a while. Then it dawned on me that the agonized hours of waiting last night must have triggered her childhood memory of the event ten years ago, when people brought back her parents' bloody bodies from the treacherous mountains! "Yes, indeed, it is dangerous in the mountains!" I choked on my own words, and I ran after her and told her that I was sorry.

After saying goodbye to Lotus, Grandmaster and I loaded two large bags of ginseng onto the horse cart, and headed toward the marketplace. On our way, Grandmaster pointed out that selling is an art of dealing with people and one must care about others by thinking more about them. He went on to tell me the following story: "There was a rich man who was eating a large piece of meat at his comfortable home when it started to snow. The rich man, wearing expensive leather clothes from head to toe, put down his meat and commented happily, 'Falling snow, how beautiful!' He turned around and asked his servant, 'My loyal servant, why is it so warm when it snows? It feels like springtime, doesn't it?' The servant, who was wearing worn-out clothes, nodded even though he was shivering with cold. Contented and pleased with his observation, the rich man turned back and continued to eat his meat." Grandmaster finished his story and asked, "Yee, what do you think about the rich man in the story?"

"I think he was very selfish and narrow-minded," I replied.

"You are right, Yee. However, do you realize that, on many occasions, we all behave just like the rich man? The rich man could afford to ignore the feelings of his poor servant because he did not rely on his servant to make a living. But in most cases, we rely on each other for support; if we think only of ourselves, we will have difficulty in making friends and finding buyers in the marketplace."

I remained quiet the rest of the way as I was contemplating the meaning of Grandmaster's teachings. When we reached the marketplace, we were among the earliest arrivals. We chose two busy areas in which to set up our stalls, opposite to each other on the same street. Grandmaster showed me how to display the ginseng so they would be more attractive.

"Yee, you must learn to sell by selling. I will go to the other side of the street to set up my display. If you need me," Grandmaster suddenly stopped talking, and pointed to a man standing across the street. "Yee, look at that old man dressed in a dark silk dress. His nickname is the Pious Monk. Do not be fooled by him."

"How come?"

"He takes advantage of people's automatic behavior. When people see a person dressed like a holy man, the majority will automatically believe that such a person is honest and immediately lower their guard. This old man dresses up as a devoted monk and acts accordingly. When people treat him with respect, he then sweet-talks them into paying tribute to Heaven and takes their goods."

"How do you know, Grandmaster?"

"When I was young and inexperienced, I was taken in by this same man." Grandmaster shrugged his shoulders.

"Is he still around after all these years?" surprised, I asked.

"As long as he is able to walk and there are people around selling goods, I guess so." Grandmaster laughed loudly. The dishonest man looked in our direction and immediately disappeared into the crowd.

"Grandmaster, why do some people still believe in the Pious Monk?" I asked.

"Don't you remember that our mind has two parts, one yin and one yang? Even though our yang mind laughs at him, our yin mind wants to believe him. Our minds become vulnerable when a person talks to us about Heaven. Some people merely want to have peace of mind by giving their goods to this dishonorable man in case he turns out to be what he claims. The marketplace is like the mountain--full of predators. Fortunately most people are honest, but always keep a vigilant eye for impostors who might come your way. Now, I am going to set up my display; just wave if you need me." Grandmaster went across the street.

As more vendors claimed their spots and spread their goods onto their stalls, I noticed that many of them were hawking about the same things. Though there were many customers buying, there were even more vendors offering them for sale. Each vendor attempted to outshout the others, proclaiming that his goods were the best in the world.

When customers came to look at my ginseng, they either complained about the price or found fault with my product. Becoming irritated, I argued with them and would point out their ignorance. Even though I won all the arguments, I did not sell a single ginseng. From time to time I glanced at Grandmaster on the other side of the street and found that his pile of ginseng was becoming smaller and smaller. Finally he sold his last bundle and came over to me.

"Not much luck today, uh?" Grandmaster said, looking at my pile of unsold ginseng.

"Grandmaster, why are they not selling?" I asked in a low voice.

"Yee, where is your enthusiasm?" Grandmaster hinted.

When I realized how emotionally upset I was by the never-ending rejections of sales, I decided to practice what Grandmaster had taught me yesterday. Instantly I put a smile on my face.

"That's better," said Grandmaster. "Yee, if you have a choice, would you rather be around cheerful people or gloomy people?"

"Cheerful people, of course."

"Were your potential customers cheerful or gloomy?"

I was now reminded that the majority of them had had a challenging attitude, which made them seem very unpleasant.

"Most of them were gloomy and sour," I answered.

"So they made you gloomy and sour?"

I lowered my head because I realized I had been discomposed by my customers. I had been very cheerful when I first started selling but gradually each customer took a piece of my cheerfulness away until there was nothing left except gloom.

Grandmaster continued, "People like to associate with others who are cheerful and enthusiastic. However, most people we meet every day lack cheerfulness and enthusiasm. When you interact with a gloomy person, there develops a battle in which either you cheer him up or he drags you down. In terms of selling, this means a sale or not a sale."

When I told Grandmaster about my arguments with my customers, he asked me, "What do you do in Tai Chi when your opponent attacks you with great force?"

"I neutralize his great force with great softness and uproot his balance."

"In the marketplace, when a customer attacks your product with negative behavior what should you do?"

"I should neutralize his negative behavior and uproot him with positive behavior?" Then I came to realize I had been doing the very opposite: I had argued with them whenever they criticized my product.

"Good! Now begin to sell again. I am going to visit some of my friends in town and I'll be back before it gets dark," said Grandmaster as he left.

With renewed enthusiasm, I began to sell again. However, I was still unable to sell anything for a long time. Many customers had bought from my competitors and had left the marketplace, leaving only a few choosy, tough customers. When a gloomy old woman came to my stall, I knew what to expect. She picked up one ginseng root, threw it back; picked up another and did the same, saying "Your ginseng is no good!" My first reaction was "How do you know? You mean old woman!"

When I realized that I was using force against force, I changed my tactics and treated the sale as a Tai Chi challenge. Accordingly, I changed my attitude and neutralized her attack by agreeing with her, saying "I know what you mean," for I knew the true purpose of her words was to make a good deal for herself. I picked up one of our best ginseng roots and said, "Look at this great ginseng: It has a head, two hands and two legs. It looks just like a living human, doesn't it? A ginseng which resembles a human body is the best ginseng, isn't it?"

She nodded, and nodded again. I was excited and tried to close the deal by putting a bunch of ginseng on the scale, asking, "Are these enough for you, lady?" Unexpectedly she said, "Wait a minute. I'm not going to buy. Your price is way too high."

My first reaction was that this woman must be a miser, but I immediately recognized that I was opposing her negative attitude with a negative attitude of my own. So I commented, "Good things are usually worth more." Then waving the ginseng enthusiastically, I tried once more, saying "Rare quality ginseng like these will give your family the very best benefits, won't they?" She nodded.

However, she decided not to buy and started to leave. Strangely I did not feel resentful and said these words from my heart, "Lady, thank you for your interest in our ginseng! Heaven bless you and your loved ones!" For I felt she might have someone sick at home.

Greatly touched by my words, she turned around and said, "Thank you, young vendor. I have been cursed by all the vendors I talked to today. I am sorry if I seemed rude; but I just couldn't help it when I thought of my ailing husband at home." Her eyes turned red as she left.

Soon afterward, two men came over and bought all my ginseng without even bargaining! After they had paid, I asked them what had made them decide to buy my ginseng. They told me that they were the servants of the lady who had just visited my stall and she had told them to buy my ginseng. The two men boasted that she was the richest lady in the neighboring five counties!

When Grandmaster came back from visiting his friends, I shouted, "Grandmaster, I have sold all the ginseng!" Grandmaster nodded as if he had expected me to do so, for he knew that strong teachers have no weak students.

We gathered our empty bags and headed home in our horse cart. When we passed through the marketplace I noticed there were still hundreds of vendors trying desperately to sell their goods. Then I realized most customers had bought from only a few vendors even though many vendors were selling the same product at more or less the same price.

"Grandmaster, many of the vendors have unsold ginseng. I feel lucky today, but I am sure that next time it will be their turn to sell out. Look at their smiling faces and note their enthusiastic attitudes--even a customer with a heart of stone will become soft and buy from them." Halfway through the marketplace, I made the comment.

"Yee, you are right that most customers have bought from only a few vendors today. But 'luck' was not the reason that they had sold all their goods today. If luck plays an important role, how is it that the same sellers sell out every day, while others do not?"

"Grandmaster, don't most of the sellers work hard, know their products, understand their customers, and approach their prospects with a cheerful manner and gung ho attitude?"

"Yee, the qualities you have just mentioned will enable a person to enter the rank of sellers. Yet only a few will break through the rank of sellers and elevate themselves to the rank of artists of selling."

"Grandmaster, what are their secrets?"

"There is only one secret and it is the same as the secret of the Tai Chi Push Hands exercise," Grandmaster answered as we passed the last seller in the marketplace. "Tell me, Yee, what is the most important principle in the Push Hands exercise? And what is the common misinterpretation of the principle?"

I knew the answer well and replied, "The primary principle is to follow my opponent's intentions by *forgetting* my own so I can use his force for my own purpose. And the common mistake is to follow my opponent's intentions by *concentrating* on my own, giving my opponent a chance to use my own force to achieve his purpose." Then I remembered my own successful sale: When I forgot my own interests and focused on genuinely treating the rich lady well, she reciprocated by treating me better than other sellers and buying from me. By forgetting my own intentions, I had actually induced her to give me what I wanted!

Grandmaster reinforced my understanding of the principle of selling when he said, "Most sellers did not sell many ginseng today because they concentrated on their own interests. Even though they understood their customers' intentions, they were too busy thinking about their own gains instead of thinking sincerely about their customers' needs. As a result, their customers did not buy from them but bought from someone who had treated them as individuals, and not merely as another sale. In fact, they had bought chiefly from their 'friends.'"

Then I recalled that Grandmaster actually had many friends in the marketplace. Indeed, his customers had become his friends for life because Grandmaster had treated them affectionately; the customers in turn had recognized this rare quality in him and had gladly become his customers and friends.

On our way home, we passed through some rice paddies. Some of them were well taken care of while others were not. Grandmaster pointed to them and said, "These fields belong to two brothers: One can lead his laborers to do good work while the other cannot. I know them well. They inherited the same amount of wealth from their father; both are very intelligent and good persons. Yet one has brought out the best in his laborers while the other has not. The art of leading is the same as the art of selling."

"But, Grandmaster, there are only two people involved in selling--a seller and his customer. However, a landlord has many laborers to oversee. How can they be the same?"

"You can bring out the best collective efforts of a thousand people by motivating the individuals around you, one by one, just like in selling. Those close to you will spread the word about the way you have been treating them to others whom you have never met. Have you heard of the Legendary Leader?"

"Yes, I understand that he was a brilliant strategist and very brave. He was frequently in the front line with his soldiers, and was devoted to his cause, often working days on end without proper sleep."

"By being brilliant, brave, and devoted, a person can enter the rank of generals. Yet only a few generals can become great leaders."

"What makes them great, Grandmaster?"

"The same principle as in selling. What a general wants is victory, but it is the people he leads who bring him victories. So a great general treats his subordinates as more important than victories in order to bring out the best in them.

"The Legendary Leader knew the principle well--whenever his men came back from a battle, the first thing he asked was how many 'brothers' had sacrificed their lives instead of asking how much land they had conquered for him. Thus, his soldiers knew he cared about their lives more than he cared about his own glory and they were more than willing to follow his orders.

"On one occasion after a victory, the Legendary Leader toured the battleground and found an old woman crying profusely. 'Aunt, why are you crying?' he inquired. She pointed to her living room where lay the bodies of her two sons who were recently killed on the battlefield. After finding out that the lady had lost five sons for his cause, this iron general cried as if he had lost his own sons. The story of this incident spread like wildfire through all the rank and file of his forces. They all knew now that the general treated them as family members. So they went after their enemies with an avenging spirit because of the loss of their 'brothers.' As a result, they gained victory after victory for the general, making him the greatest general of all time." Grandmaster finished his story, and I kept quiet for the rest of the journey, contemplating the essence of what he had said.

When we arrived at the Chen Village, the sun was setting as a big fireball on the horizon. The whole world was suffused with a beautiful red color--the houses were red, the haystacks were red, the fences were red, the pigs, hens, and cows were all red. I was standing on high ground, admiring the distant rice paddies and the fields of corn and yams as they all basked in this wonderful twilight. The mountain stream was reflecting the color of the setting sun and had become a red river, as if it was celebrating the last brilliant sunlight of the day. This poem came to my mind:

> As the day approaches the end I become restless,
> I ride in a horse carriage to an old grassy knoll;
> The sunset is so boundlessly beautiful,
> I only regret it is approaching its end.

There was an old temple in the distance, standing against this magnificent setting sun as it had been doing for the last few centuries. Yes, the temple might have seen it all, but it was still contentedly witnessing this incredibly beautiful show. Birds hurrying back to their nests slowed their pace to give thanks to the sun for the warmth it had given them today. As my eyes followed the birds flying behind me, I saw my long shadow cast on the ground, blending perfectly with my surroundings.

The barking of the dog at Grandmaster's house finally reminded me that I had not seen Lotus since I had returned from the marketplace. So I went to see her immediately and found her unhappy. Her expression was serious and she even appeared to be in a state of melancholy. With a smiling face, I tried to cheer her up, but she remained unimpressed.

At first I blamed myself for having been so insensitive this morning. Then when she continued to be sulky, it affected me and soon I became unhappy myself. I started to wonder, Why doesn't she learn to control her mood? Why is she so immature? Why can't she be cheerful?

I wanted desperately for Lotus to come out of her unpleasant mood so we could both be happy again. However, without a word, Lotus headed toward the Reflecting Pond and I followed her.

By now, the sun had already gone down into the distant mountains and the moon had become visible. The wind was blowing strongly. Like my unsettled mind, the water in the Reflecting Pond was rough and disturbed. Lotus and I sat down next to each other, with Lotus still in her unpleasant state of mind, and I still asking myself why. Then I heard a night bird crying and it sounded as if it were saying "Selling! Selling!"

Selling? Suddenly it dawned on me that the art of dealing with people was just the same as the art of selling, and I had made the common mistake of concentrating on my own feelings instead of trying to understand the other person. First, I blamed myself for being insensitive toward Lotus; then I blamed Lotus for creating the unhappy environment which had made me so miserable.

So instead of concentrating on how the situation was affecting me, I began to appreciate Lotus as a human being, entitled to have her own moody moments. As my attitude was transformed from that of challenging to one of understanding and compassion, my body expression correspondingly changed from one of coldness to one of warmth and love.

The instant that my eyes met her eyes again, we became one for that brief moment. I glimpsed deeply into her soul and saw that Lotus wanted to make me happy just as I wanted to make her happy; and if she could have helped herself she would have done everything to please me, for she knew that I would have done the same for her. Without a word being exchanged, a big smile came across her face as she took hold of my hands and said, "Yee, I am sorry for having made you feel so bad today."

"Indeed, I am sorry for neglecting you today, Lotus. I love you." Just when the yin and yang attraction became strong and as I drew close to her, Grandmaster called for Lotus and we left the pond immediately.

When I returned to my room, I could not fall asleep. The watchman had already struck the midnight hour but I was still wide awake. I put on some clothes and left for the Reflecting Pond again. When I arrived, the moon had already passed midheaven and the wind had died down.

I was once again alone, facing the Reflecting Pond. Images of the people I had met today appeared in my mind: customers and vendors, the rich lady and her servants, Grandmaster and Lotus. When I was still in my own village, could I have dreamed that one day I would meet all those people? How, among millions and millions of people out there, could we have met today? Maybe it was fated or maybe it was pure chance, but in either case, the people I had met today ought to be special to me. But if this was so, why didn't I feel special when I was with them? Maybe I was thinking that some of them I would only meet this one time and never again in my life? Or maybe I was thinking that some of them I would meet daily and that they would always be around?

Then I remembered to look at the possibilities which life has to offer. If life is full of possibilities, why should I treat people as strangers when there is a possibility that we will meet again? And why should I take it for granted that those people I meet every day will always be around, when there is a possibility that we might never meet again?

Looking at the moonlight reflected in the calm water, I found myself talking to all the people I have met and will meet during my lifetime, "You might have hurt me, laughed at me, and made my life miserable, or you might have helped me, encouraged me, and made my life worth living. Whatever role you have played in my life, isn't our encounter still special since the chance of our meeting in this lifetime is one in a million? So for those I have already met, I say thank you for the experience we have shared. For those whom I am going to meet every day and those only once in my lifetime, I will greet you with love in my heart."

Gradually my mind became as quiet and as soft as the moonlight on the Reflecting Pond. I felt an urge to close my eyes and look inside myself. When I did, I was surprised to find myself empty. Why couldn't I concentrate on myself? Was I telling myself that to love myself, I must love others first by concentrating on them and forgetting myself?

I pondered further: If I can love others first, just like the Legendary Leader has done, am I not a source of inspiration, a leader, and a person of great responsibility? Suddenly I felt a rush of energy going through my body; I raised my hands high and ran under the moonlight, shouting, "Yes, I can be a source of inspiration! I am a leader! I am a man of great responsibility! The world is heavy but I can carry it! Yes, I can carry the world on my shoulders!"

While I was as excited as a man on the top of the world, I realized there was another side of me. It was trying to keep me in balance, saying: Put your world down! Go to the world of happy thoughts! Go to the world of possibilities! Have fun and excitement now! Have fun and excitement now!

When the yang world of responsibility and the yin world of possibility fused together to form a perfect Tai Chi Circle within me, I felt the ease and joy of carrying the two worlds on my shoulders simultaneously, for when two equally heavy worlds, with one negative and one positive, add up, there is no weight. A delighted smile came to my face as I realized this was indeed, the Third Secret of the Tai Chi Circle.

The secret has become a part of my thinking as I welcome each day with these happy thoughts:

Hello sunshine, fragrant flowers, and smiling faces, I am in love! Today, I concentrate on the needs of others, for to love others is to love myself.

Hello sunshine, fragrant flowers, and smiling faces, I am in love! Today, I concentrate on the needs of others, for to love others is to love myself.

Hello sunshine, fragrant flowers, and smiling faces, I am in love! Today, I concentrate on the needs of others, for to love others is to love myself.

Chapter Five

Blue Sky

One day when I was practicing my Tai Chi movements, I noticed an old gentleman with silver hair watching me with curious eyes. I stopped my practice and asked respectfully, "May I help you, Sir?"

He nodded his head to acknowledge my question and laughed gently but said nothing. He walked away slowly reciting a poem:

"I left my hometown as a youth and returned as an old man.

My dialect has not changed but my hair has turned gray;

Children whom I met on my way home did not know me.

With smiling faces they asked me, 'Where are you coming from, stranger?'"

I was puzzled and wondered who this gentleman might be. After a while I saw Lotus running excitedly toward me, shouting, "Great-Grandpa is back!"

"Grandmaster's father is still alive? How old is he?" I asked excitedly.

"He is eighty-seven years old," replied Lotus, taking my hand. "Come, Yee. Let's go and see Great-Grandpa. He always has interesting stories to tell." I agreed and we left to see him immediately.

We arrived at Great-Grandmaster's house, which was in the center of the village, and found him writing at his desk. I noticed a large painting hanging conspicuously in his room. The painting depicted a group of happy people waving their hands as if they were bidding farewell to someone, and in the background a beautiful scene disclosing a village surrounded by mountains. Underneath the painting were these words:

Through the mist there seemed to be a narrow passageway.

I walked close to the shore and asked a gentleman in a boat:

When peach flowers mature they follow the river;

But where is the entrance to the cave of this paradise?

"Please come in. I am so glad you young people have come to see

59

me," Great-Grandmaster greeted us happily and beckoned us to sit. "I am happy that the jade plate has been united, Yee. Please tell me all about yourself and about the village you came from."

I talked on excitedly as Great-Grandmaster was such a good listener--he listened to me as if I were the only person in the world. He nodded his head from time to time to acknowledge that he understood my words. His penetrating eyes assured me that he comprehended every syllable I uttered. What a wonderful feeling--being listened to like this!

When I finished, he said, "It was very interesting, Yee. I have learned something from you today. Thank you."

"Indeed, thank you for listening to me, sir. I like you very much." Great-Grandmaster had already gained my respect and trust merely by listening to me this one time!

"Sir, does this picture represent your goal?" I pointed to the picture over his desk.

Knowing his son had taught me how to set up goals, he smiled and said, "Yes. If you are interested, I will tell you the story behind this painting." Lotus and I nodded our heads immediately.

Great-Grandmaster began, "One day I was taking a trip in a small boat on a stream which I had discovered the day before. It was an exceptionally beautiful day with birds singing high in the trees and flowers everywhere. I rowed my boat gently up stream while I admired the peach trees on either side which were blossoming with beautiful white and red flowers. As the wind blew, the flowers fell gently onto the water and floated slowly downstream. The stream meandered through a mountainous region and became narrower and narrower as it approached its water source. I was so happy to see such beautiful scenery that I almost forgot where I was. When I reached a narrow area where I could row no further, I returned home reluctantly.

"That night I had a dream. In my dream, I returned to where I had broken off my adventure during the day and discovered a small passage just wide enough for my boat to pass through. After I rowed on for some time, the passage led my boat into an underground water cave. I rowed on and reached the opening at the other end of the cave; I soon found that this exit was hidden on the outside under the roots of a huge tree.

"I climbed up the roots, looked around, and saw that I had reached an area full of beautiful peach trees. Just as I became excited by my discovery, I stepped onto a dead root and fell down heavily, struck my head, and lost consciousness. When I regained my senses, I found myself in the hands of a kindly looking woman, who was feeding me.

'Where am I, Aunt?' I whispered, feeling rather weak.

'Welcome to Peach Flower Garden, my son,' she replied with a smile and continued to nurture me as a mother would do. She carefully fed me warm food one spoonful at a time and patiently wiped off drops of food which had fallen on my clothes. I was truly moved by her kindness and asked, 'Aunt, I am but a stranger, why do you treat me with so much love?'

'My son, in Peach Flower Garden, we are all mothers and sons, brothers and sisters. Now have a good night's sleep. Tomorrow you will be yourself again.' She hummed a sweet song for me while she untied her head towel and used it to give me warmth. I noticed a beautiful red peach flower embroidered in the towel and I felt so much love and peace while under this flower of love that I soon fell sound asleep.

"Early next morning, at the first cock crow, I was awakened by the commotion of the village people as they were getting up. They were already on the move when the first ray of sun struck. I looked through the window and saw young couples cheerfully carrying their hoes to cultivate the land while the old were happily taking care of their young. I heard people address the lady who nurtured me last night as 'Grandmother.'

"When people settled down to their duties, I asked, 'Grandmother, why are people so excited and happy today?'

'Today is a special day, my son,' she answered and showed me the children she was taking care of.

"Seeing her treating all the children alike, I asked, 'Grandmother, are all those children your grandchildren?'

'Well, I have only two. Four of them belong to our neighbors whose grandparents passed away last summer. The rest are orphans,' Grandmother answered.

'How many baskets of rice do they give you for your service?' I asked, thinking that she must earn a good living by providing care for other families.

'My son, here in Peach Flower Garden, we help each other without obligations. Good deeds come around in circles and they will return to those who help others. One family gives help in one way and will receive help in another way. In the long run, each family will give and get help from others equally,' Grandmother answered.

'But, Grandmother, how can a permanently disabled person give and receive equal help from others?' I asked, thinking that even this paradise must have its share of unfortunates.

'My son, a disabled head of a household might be incapable of giving help himself. But his ancestors had probably helped ours and his descendants will help ours in case they become disabled. Here in Peach Flower Garden, we love the strong and the weak, the clever and the foolish, the beautiful and the ugly, the rich and the poor. If we only love the strong, the clever, the beautiful, and the rich, our love will not be a complete love, for the things we love cannot exist without the weak, the foolish, the ugly, and the poor. My son, you are in a place of love.' After saying that, Grandmother proceeded with her busy day of taking care of the children.

"The news of a visitor coming to the village had spread quickly and people were coming in from all directions to greet me. At first, I thought the villagers were actors and actresses because they were wearing ancient garments which could have been seen only in plays. They seemed to be even more curious about the way I was dressed. Some children came close to me and touched my clothes and held my hands. When the adults started to talk, I soon realized that their language was only to be found in the classics. I wanted to talk to Grandmother because I could not communicate with these people but she was nowhere to be found. I finally decided to recite a poem from each dynasty to see which they could understand.

"They all laughed and started to hug me when I recited the poem from the Tang Dynasty:

"Since you were from my hometown,
You ought to know the current events there:
The day you left your decorated window,
Have the plum trees begun to blossom as yet?"

"Soon I found out that their ancestors had come to this land centuries ago to escape famine created by ceaseless wars. Since then they had lost contact with the outside world. They had not known of the existence of Song, Yuan, Ming, and Ching Dynasties. Indeed, they had been living in peace while millions and millions of people outside were being killed through disease, famine, and wars whenever one dynasty overthrew another.

"The people cheerfully showed me their village, and I found that this paradise was a place of plenty. Fruit trees were everywhere; rivers were teeming with fish; mountains were covered with tall trees and were full of game animals. The soil was so fertile that plants grew rapidly without requiring much human effort. Famine was unknown here so no one was trying greedily to accumulate more food than they actually needed. Crime was also unknown here so nobody put locks on their doors. They were all happy and contented people.

"As night fell again, I came back to Grandmother who put me up comfortably for the night. Next morning, I was again awakened by the same excited people welcoming the first cock crow. It was obvious to me that everyone in this village was eager to get up to welcome a new day. When I saw Grandmother's smiling face again, I asked, 'Grandmother, what is the occasion today? Why are people so fully alert and energetic?'

'My son, today is a special day.'

'Again?'

'Yes, again, my son. Indeed, in Peach Flower Garden, every day is a special day,' she answered in a loving voice.

'Why is that?'

'Today is a special day because we all are one day younger than tomorrow. We are looking forward to finishing our daily work today and to going on to new things. This is a lovely day, my son.'

'But Grandmother, why don't outsiders feel they are younger today than tomorrow?'

'My son, even as a child, people already feel old when a new sibling is born, and their parents pay more attention to the newborn. An attractive lady of seventeen, the fairest of all, still feels old when she sees her fifteen-year-old sister ready to blossom into a beautiful flower. Remember, my son, no matter how young a person is, a new generation will always come up to replace her. Being old is only in one's mind, my son.'

'Grandmother, why do people here feel so young?'

'My son, in Peach Flower Garden, there is no envy but only love. We are content with what we have and are happy for what others have. We do not compare things among ourselves. We only know that yesterday has gone forever and today we are younger than we will be the rest of the days of our lives. We celebrate our youth together.' After saying that, Grandmother left to fetch water for her children.

"It finally dawned on me that I was indeed one day younger than tomorrow. I ran outside and saw the sun just coming up beyond the distant mountains. Birds, insects, animals, grass, bushes, trees, all seemed to know that they, too, are one day younger than tomorrow and joined in to celebrate today. I raised my hands high and shouted, 'Thank you for giving me a new day. I love you, Today! I love you!' I felt so excited that I wanted to leave immediately to tell the outside world about this place of love.

"After bidding Grandmother goodbye, I was ready to go home. By the time I left, all the village people lined up to bid me goodbye and asked me to come back as soon as possible. Yet none of them seemed interested in how I had gotten there and nobody followed me when I reached the entrance to the cave. I took the same route back to our own village. There it was that I woke up from my dream."

"What happened next?" Lotus asked.

Great-Grandmaster continued, "I immediately took the same route back to the water source as the day before, wishing that my dream could come true. But I could not find the entrance to the cave I had dreamed about. Why did I dream about meeting people and traveling to new places? Could it be my hidden desire to learn from the outside world in order to improve my mind? I wondered and then remembered that one time my father had said to me, 'My son, developing our mind is Tai Chi. Listening to people and traveling to new places will develop our minds. When two minds come together, a third mind is born. A new environment can also stimulate our mind and give us inspiration. If we can surround ourselves with diverse people and change our environment often, our minds can function better as we grow older. If we do not feed new ideas into our mind, it will be less functional, just like our body which loses its strength as we grow old.' I realized that my father and my dream were telling me to meet people and learn.

"So from that time onward, I woke up at the first cock crow and quickly finished my assigned work, and went out to meet people and do new things. Soon I realized the best way to learn from people is to listen carefully to what they are saying to me. People love to talk about themselves and I can make friends with them by just listening to them instead of talking about my own interests."

"Why do people love to talk about themselves but are reluctant to listen to others?" Lotus asked.

"People prefer talking over listening because talking does not require much effort while listening requires much discipline. When people talk about themselves, they are talking about something they already know. However, when people listen to others, they are learning something new. If one can suppress one's natural tendency to talk about oneself ceaselessly, and cultivate the ability to listen to others, one will find oneself above others like a 'crane standing among chickens.'"

"What happened next, Sir?" I was curious to know.

Great-Grandmaster continued, "After I had my dream, I became restless. I wanted to travel afar but was afraid my father would disapprove of my absence here. My father noticed my uneasiness during a Tai Chi session and asked what was bothering me. I told him I wanted to travel and learn things from the outside world. He patted me on the back and said, 'Follow your dreams, my son. I know you will be successful and bring back much new knowledge to our village.'

"So I began to travel to many places and meet many people. Each time I traveled I brought back new inventions from the outside to improve our own method of farming. I also introduced new crops such as tomatoes to our village. Indeed, I became very useful to our village people."

"Great Grandpa, do you still hope to find your paradise?" Lotus asked.

"Yes, I will follow my dream till the end of time," Great-Grandmaster replied.

Just when we had thanked Great-Grandmaster for telling us his story, we heard some strange sounds coming from upstairs.

"What's the noise?" I asked.

"I guess my father is calling for me," Great-Grandmaster replied.

"Your *father?*" I stared at him in disbelief.

Lotus giggled and said apologetically, "Yee, I forgot to tell you about my Great-Great-Grandpa, who lives upstairs."

How old is he?"

He will be celebrating his one-hundred-and-third birthday next month!" Lotus replied.

We found that Great-Great-Grandmaster was calling for us, so Lotus and I went upstairs to see him. He was sitting in a chair with a book in his hands. His body was thin but his eyes penetrated mine like those of a true Tai Chi master. I noted that he was surrounded by books.

"Yee, I am glad to see you," he greeted me enthusiastically.

"Sir, I am sorry that I have not visited you earlier. I feel honored that you know my name." I was surprised that he knew it.

"Young people have other priorities," he commented, looking in Lotus's direction.

"Sir, you have a lot of books. Have you read all of them?"

"Yes. Some of them many times."

Then I noticed a large picture hung over his bookshelf. It showed a large frog jumping upward into the sky from a large water pond.

"Can you tell me the meaning of this painting?" I asked.

"Please sit. I will tell you about it," replied the old master, and Lotus and I sat next to him.

Suddenly we heard some strange sound up in the attic. "It must be my Moa. She is getting hungry," said Great-Great-Grandmaster.

"YOUR MOM?" I gasped, with my eyes opened wide.

"No, what's wrong with you, Yee? It was my Moa, the cat," Great-Great-Grandmaster said seriously.

I saw Lotus put a hand on her mouth, muffling her laugh.

"I am sorry, sir. I was just joking. Please tell us the story," I apologized.

He began, "This picture depicts my goal. More accurately it represents a dream I had one night when I was a young man. I dreamed that I was a frog living in a small well. There were a few frogs living in the well at the same time. As I was the strongest, I was respected and treated as their leader.

"I thought the well was the whole world and that the world was surrounded by walls. Occasionally there were some frogs who dropped down from the sky and told me that there was a bigger world outside. Thinking they were ignorant, I never bothered to investigate their claims.

"One day it rained heavily and the well almost filled up. One of the frogs, which had recently dropped down from above, kept trying to jump out of the well, until he became exhausted. He came to me and begged, 'Great Leader, you are the strongest of all of us and only you have the strength to jump out of this well to freedom. Please jump to freedom before it is too late.' I laughed at him and said, 'Why are you so stubborn, old frog? There is no bigger sky out there. Even if there were one, I am perfectly happy here.'

'Our Great Leader, please believe me. It is a wonderful world out there if you can jump out of this one. These walls are limiting your freedom, Great Leader!' the old frog begged me again.

'Why are you so stupid, old frog? Can't you see there is no bigger world outside? We are only frogs; we belong here. Be contented with what you are and where you are and please bother me no more.'

"The water level became lower again as the rainy season passed. However, one night there was an unusually heavy rainfall during the dry season and the well swelled again. There was a beetle, in the wrong place at the wrong time, who was washed down into the well. Unfamiliar with the rules of the well and being hungry, the beetle searched everywhere for food. When it swam close to me, thinking I was dead because I was just floating there doing nothing, it took a big bite out of me. It hurt so much that I jumped high and found myself out of the well!

"I could not believe my eyes. There was actually a bigger world outside! I saw a beautiful rainbow hanging over the endless sky. There were trees and mountains I had never known before. Then I saw a big pond in front of me and I was so happy that I jumped right into it. It was the first time that I could swim freely without touching walls.

"As I slipped effortlessly through the water I saw different kinds of fish swimming by. I rose to the water surface, where I saw many dragonflies gracefully gliding over the water, and different kinds of insects dancing around enjoying themselves. Why was I so contented to have lived for so long in the tiny well locked in by the solid walls? If I had only known!

"Then I saw a large number of frogs jumping and playing among a patch of water lilies. I jumped to join them and soon learned their tricks of jumping and landing playfully. Suddenly I saw one of the frogs flash his tongue out to catch an insect for lunch. I tried the same trick and discovered I, too, had that ability!

"As night fell, the frogs gathered to hear their leader exhorting them to believe that their world was the greatest of all worlds. As the leader went on and on, I realized that he sounded more and more like me, doing what I used to do, only he had a larger audience. A thought flashed through my mind: There might be another world if we could jump out of this one. So I started to jump, jump, and jump.

"I woke up from my dream and found myself jumping up and down in my bed." Great-Great-Grandmaster came to his conclusion: "The dream was saying that I had a narrow mind and I should broaden my knowledge so I can obtain a higher level of awareness. And from that day onward I started to read books."

"Why did you choose reading?" I asked.

"If you don't read, you only know what you yourself think. Books

Zhang Yang

I could not believe my eyes. There was actually a bigger world outside!

contain great ideas from great thinkers. They help us to see the world as the great thinkers have seen it. Each time when I have finished reading a good book I feel like I have made an effort to jump out of my well of ignorance."

I could not but wonder why a person as old as Great-Great-Grandmaster kept on reading books. He seemed to have read my mind and said, "When I was young I read books to increase my knowledge so that I could become a better provider for my family. As I've grown older, reading has become a necessity for me. It is no longer a luxury. Now the purpose of my reading is to stay alive. As you can see, my body has almost completely deteriorated; the only thing I have left is my mind. I must keep it alive by stimulating it."

I became interested in finding out more about his daily life, so I asked, "Sir, you have obtained a long and happy life as promised in Tai Chi. Do you still practice the Tai Chi exercise every day?"

"Yes. I do it using my mind. I don't need to move my body very much. Now whenever I think about my Tai Chi movements, the life energy will spread through my body, keeping me healthy. Meanwhile, I still keep on dreaming about my goal. One day you will understand the true meaning of my goal and why I am trying to jump out of this world."

After finishing, he handed me a book and asked me to read it aloud for him. The book was a collection of poetry. I opened it and read the first poem, entitled "On Reading."

"This half acre pond opens like a mirror,
Reflections of the sky and clouds are lingering there;
How can it become so clear and bright?
Because sources of streams keep pouring in."

When I finished, I saw Lotus signaling me to keep quiet. Great-Great-Grandmaster had just fallen asleep in his comfortable chair.

We tiptoed downstairs.

"Yee, you are such a good reader!" Lotus teased and ran.

"What do you mean?" I chased after her.

When we stepped out of the house, I took a deep breath and proclaimed, "Lotus, look at the blue sky, it is smaller than it was before we had entered the house."

"To the contrary, I think the sky is bigger than before," replied Lotus.

"Why are you saying that, Lotus? Haven't you learned anything after talking to the great masters?"

"The size of the sky has nothing to do with the great masters, Yee. After people stay in a room bounded by walls for a long time and go out into the open, people would naturally feel they are in much bigger place." She tried to convince me.

"How we estimate the size of the sky is influenced by our mind, Lotus. Since our minds have been expanded after hearing the story of the frog, we should think this sky is not a big one." I tried to educate her.

"Yee, you are right that how we estimate the size of the sky is influenced by our mind. But remember our mind is first influenced by our body's feelings. Our body should feel the sky is bigger since we just came out from a small place," she argued.

"The sky is smaller. Use your mind, Lotus." I tried to be patient.

"The sky is bigger. Trust your feelings, Yee." Lotus was trying to be patient with me too.

"The sky is smaller. Why are you so stubborn?" I raised my voice a little bit.

"The sky is bigger and that is that. I am not talking to you anymore." Lotus lost her patience too and walked faster.

I became desperate and shouted, "The sky is smaller. Why are you so STUPID?"

After hearing my words, Lotus began to run toward the Reflecting Pond, and I followed her. When we reached the pond she reduced her speed to a walking pace. Instead of following her, I walked the other way.

The day had progressed into a beautiful evening as the sun disappeared behind the distant mountains. Soon the moon appeared in the sky and its shadow was reflected on the perfectly calm pond. The moonlight fell softly on the treetops, casting long shadows on the water surface. A few night birds fluttered by and everything seemed to exist in perfect harmony.

I looked at the smooth water surface and saw the shadow of Lotus sitting on the opposite side of the pond, with her head down, deep in thought. Why are you so obstinate, Lotus? I stared at her shadow and shook my head. Suddenly I heard a frog croaking at the edge of the pond and I walked toward it. Hearing my footsteps, the frog jumped high into the air before disappearing in the pond with a splash.

The frog reminded me of the lesson I had learned today and it hit me like lightning: Am I not also obstinate? Don't I realize that I am living like a frog in a well, surrounded by walls of ignorance? Why is my mind so narrow that I cannot hold one more idea arising from my beloved Lotus? If, like the spear and the shield, two opposing ideas can coexist as long as they are not used against each other, why do I still insist I am right and she is wrong? But in the end, don't both of us get hurt emotionally? When will I ever learn? I felt ashamed and covered my head with both hands.

After a while, I felt a hand touching my shoulder. I turned around and found Lotus near me.

"Did you hear the frog croaking from my side of the pond?" she asked.

"No, the one I heard was from my side of the pond," I replied.

I held her hands and said, "Lotus, how can we stop quarreling over petty things?"

"We need to develop our minds."

"What is the best way to develop our minds?" I asked.

"I think listening to people and going places is the best way," Lotus replied.

"No, I believe reading books is better," I disagreed.

"No, listening to people and going places," she insisted.

"No, reading books." I would not budge.

Then we looked at each other and realized we were arguing again.

"Listening to people, going places, and reading books," we said simultaneously and laughed.

We had reached a better understanding of ourselves and were glad we had each other to learn life's lessons from. We held hands as we walked back to the house.

After Lotus said goodnight and went to her room, I had the urge to return to the Reflecting Pond. When I did, I found the Pond was as smooth as a sheet of glass. In front of this deep and serene natural pond, I pondered the lessons I had learned from the great masters today. Am I one day younger than tomorrow? Why is it that being young is such an exciting thing? Is it because a young person, like a young plant coming up from the ground and sprouting new leaves, is growing and learning new things every day and, therefore, always has something to look forward to in life?

Then I thought about the lessons in terms of yin and yang. When I view my existence as being joyful and young, I am looking at my life from the viewpoint of myself; this is subjective and yin. But when I detach myself from my own small world by meeting people, going places, and reading books, I see my life from the viewpoint of an outsider; this is objective and yang.

So one side of me chose to live in my own world of being young, curious, and always growing and learning while the other side of me detached myself from my own world, seeing my life just as it was-- having the same sorrows and joys as other individuals. In my own world, I was a child, always growing; out of my own world, I was an adult, always sharing. Finally when these two sides fused into a perfect Tai Chi Circle within me, I felt as though the water source of the pond had been connected to my body, and my mind became as clear and open as the Reflecting Pond itself. Indeed, the Fourth Secret of the Tai Chi Circle had just been revealed to me.

These words repeatedly arose in my mind, as if I were taking an oath to live the Secret:

Feel young, forever young, for today I am one day younger than tomorrow; jump high, high and out of the well of ignorance, for I listen to people, go places, and read books.

Feel young, forever young, for today I am one day younger than tomorrow; jump high, high and out of the well of ignorance, for I listen to people, go places, and read books.

Feel young, forever young, for today I am one day younger than tomorrow; jump high, high and out of the well of ignorance, for I listen to people, go places, and read books.

Chapter Six

Red Rose

Spring came and the earth was bustling with life again. One day Lotus and I were riding horses in the woods. When we reached the open field, I stood up on my galloping horse and performed some tricks. Lotus clapped her hands and said I was the best rider she had ever seen. I had always considered myself an excellent rider and felt very proud. But there was always a shadow of failure in my mind which I could not erase. When we finished riding, I went to the Putee Tree to take my Tai Chi lesson. Grandmaster noticed that I was not concentrating on my lesson, and asked, "Is there something on your mind that bothers you, Yee?"

"Yes, Grandmaster. Something has been troubling me for a long time and Lotus reminded me of that very thing not too long ago."

"Can you tell me about it? Perhaps I can give you some ideas."

"Yes, Grandmaster. I am still obsessed by my failure to have made our village's horse racing team five years ago. My mind had never accepted that I was a horse's head too slow to make the team on the final trial race. Now, in my dreams I still go back again and again to that race, trying to rerun it. It troubles me, Grandmaster."

Grandmaster held my hands as we sat next to each other. "Yee, we all have many failures over the years. Let me tell you an ancient story to help you to see clearly that failures are nothing to be ashamed of.

"The Headmaster of a religious order was getting old and wanted to choose a successor. He encouraged his followers to offer themselves as candidates regardless of their rankings. So, many masters and their students applied. After a long process of elimination, the Headmaster narrowed his choices to three final candidates: a master with a long beard, an ordinary looking master, and the latter's young student. These three candidates had shown all the qualities needed to be a successful headmaster. The conventional methods of choosing a successor could not differentiate them. Since only one of them could be chosen as his successor, the Headmaster came up with a novel idea to test their ability to control their minds.

"There was a beautiful pond with a small waterfall in a mountainous region not far from the head monastery. The Headmaster told the three finalists to travel to the pond and wash their bodies there. When the three candidates reached the pond and stripped down to their waists, they heard voices yelling for help and saw three beautiful maidens struggling in the water. Thinking the Headmaster was testing their courage, the candidates immediately jumped into the pond and tried to save the maidens. When they were in the water, they discovered that the maidens were naked. The bearded master held a young maiden closely to his body and carried her to safety as if she were no more than a child. But the other master and his student were physically aroused and trembled with excitement as they carried their maidens to the shore.

"When they were all safely on the shore, the bearded master smiled triumphantly because he was the only candidate who appeared successful in resisting the temptation of the flesh. It seemed clear to everyone who would be the successor to the Headmaster. They all went back to their respective monasteries to wait for the Headmaster to summon them for the official announcement of his choice.

"A few days later, the two young maidens saved by the master and his student came to the monastery and stayed briefly to give thanks to them for saving their lives.

"A month later, the official ordination ceremony was held in the head monastery. The three candidates were kneeling down in front of the Headmaster and all other masters and students were sitting around them in a semicircle. The Headmaster spoke, 'Masters and students, welcome to our special meeting. Today I will choose my successor and he will be your new leader. I hope all of you will support and respect him as you have supported and respected me over the years.'

"He turned to the three candidates and spoke, 'Three of you have reached a very high level of self-cultivation. Since only one of you will succeed to my position, I hope the remaining two will work harmoniously with your new leader.' The bearded master nodded and smiled happily while the other two finalists just nodded.

"The Headmaster turned to the bearded master and spoke, 'My fellow master, when you held the naked young maiden close to your bare body, I observed your reaction from a place above the pond and saw your mind was not affected by such a great temptation.' The bearded master was obviously pleased because the Headmaster was there to witness that he was the only one who had successfully passed the test.

"The Headmaster continued, 'However, I was suspicious of what I saw and sent out two of my entrusted followers separately to investigate how you had achieved such a high degree of mind development. They reported back to me independently that you had been taking a special herb for many years to suppress your physical desire. So your resistance to the temptation was not because of the calmness of your mind but because you were physically unable to react.' Then he raised his voice, 'My fellow master, there is no shortcut to enlightenment. The route you were taking is actually the longest one. Now go back to your monastery and repent!' The bearded master knew his secret had been revealed and quietly withdrew.

"The Headmaster then turned to the remaining two candidates and spoke, 'Between you two, I choose the master as my successor.' And he signaled his assistants to put a yellow robe on the master in order to ordain him as their new leader.

"But before they made the decision official by putting the yellow robe on his master, the student broke his silence, 'Our fair and just Headmaster, you must have seen with your own eyes that my master and I had both failed to pass the flesh test. Why do you choose him, not me?'

'My child, indeed, both you and your master have failed this human temptation. However, your master left his failure the moment he put down his naked lady. But you, my child, have been living with your failure ever since, for you are still holding your young lady.'

'Our great and intelligent Headmaster, how do you know?' The student was not so easily convinced.

'My child, I sent the ladies back to your monastery a few days later to visit you and your master. While your master received his lady like a holy man would receive his followers, you received yours in a strange way--you were afraid to look directly into her eyes. Why?' The Headmaster raised his voice, 'Because you still imagined holding her naked body. You could not get her out of your mind! Now go back to your monastery and meditate more!'

"Even though the student knew that what the Headmaster had said was true he still didn't understand why he was not chosen. So he asked boldly, 'Our merciful Headmaster, I, I at least feel ashamed because of my failure. But my master does not feel even a little bit of remorse for having failed. How can he be our leader? Besides, I am young and he is old. If I am chosen, I can lead our order for many years to come without the need of finding another successor.'

"The Headmaster looked straight into the student's eyes and asked solemnly, 'Tell me, my child, what is your real reason for wanting to become our new leader?' The words penetrated the student's soul.

"The student begged, 'The day when I left my home, I made a promise to my parents that I would become the most successful holy man in our order. I have since worked very hard to fulfill my promise. So if I fail to become one, I will feel shame, shame, shame!'

'Chain! Chain! Chain!' the Headmaster exclaimed.

'I mean shame, shame, shame, not chain, chain, chain, Headmaster.' The student tried to correct his leader.

'My child, I have heard you loud and clear. But, have you heard me? Your shame is just like a chain, keeping you as a slave in your own prison. For every failure in your life, you have added on one more chain to yourself as a prisoner. You were born as a free person but your accumulated shame has made you a slave. Whenever you want to achieve something worthwhile your shame will prevent you from even trying. As you grow older you will be burdened with so much shame that you will become a living mummy, waiting to be laid down. Haven't you seen people bound by their own chains of shame come to our monasteries every day, trying desperately for us to free them? If you yourself are bound in chains, how can you unchain them?'

"Then the Headmaster raised his stick and struck the student squarely on his head and thundered, 'DON'T YOU UNDERSTAND THAT THOSE CHAINS EXIST IN YOUR MIND ONLY? '

"The student finally understood that he was indeed, no better than the common people. So he crawled down to the feet of his Headmaster and never challenged his decision again."

After Grandmaster had finished his story, I, too, understood that I had been carrying my own chains of shame all my life. Sometimes my chains became so heavy that I could not get up to face the world. Now I knew it was all in my mind.

"Grandmaster, since we cannot avoid failure, we should take failure in stride?"

"Yes, Yee. The manner in which we deal with our failures will separate the outstanding from the ordinary. Moreover, failures might be blessings in disguise, for every event happens with a purpose."

"What do you mean, Grandmaster?"

"In order to truly understand the meaning of failure and success, you need to visit our relatives in the Village of Beauties and talk to the oldest man on earth, one-hundred-and-ten-year-old Mr. Old Cripple," Grandmaster suggested.

"How are you related to those villagers?"

"Lotus's mother was from that village."

I was extremely eager to find out the secret of Lotus's beauty. So next morning I mounted a horse and started my journey. Grandmaster and Lotus accompanied me until we reached the main road at the foot of the mountain. Grandmaster waved his hand for me to go on after he had recited this poem:

"Green mountains across the north side of the villa.
White rivers surround the East City.
Once we are apart from here,
Like a lonely boat you will sail a thousand miles.
The drifting cloud understands the feeling of a traveler.
The setting sun remembers the friendship left behind.
I wave my hands to bid you farewell.
From a distance I still hear the horses neigh."

After a long journey I finally reached the Village of Beauties. I rode along a country road lined with oak trees on both sides, and it led me to the heart of the village. There was a stream alongside the road and I saw several beautiful girls washing clothes in its crystal clear water. I was welcomed by Lotus's relatives and settled down comfortably.

That night I went out for a walk under the silvery moonlight. I strolled along the stream banks and enjoyed the sound of the running water and the chirps of the crickets. I went down the stream, scooped a handful of this cool mountain water, and refreshed myself. As I stood up, I saw a reflection of someone in the water--it must be Mr. Old Cripple, for he was very old and stood on one leg.

"Sir, I have come here to learn from your wisdom," I told him respectfully.

"Everything happens for a reason. Since you have come from a thousand miles away to see me, you must not go home empty. Let me tell you my story, and it is up to you to learn something from it."

We sat on the stream bank and he began, "When I was a young boy I was healthy and happy. I was very optimistic and believed that the future held great promise for me. Then, one day disaster struck: While riding a horse, I made a silly mistake by pulling up the horse too quickly. I fell, broke my right leg, and was rendered unconscious. When I woke up my whole world had changed--I had become a cripple.

"At first I did not think too much about it because my parents loved me so and we were a happy family. My father fixed me a crutch which helped me to walk freely. When I recovered, I walked with my crutch and visited some friends. My friends behaved very strangely and appeared reluctant to play with me because I could no longer keep up with them. When I overheard one of them referring to me as the 'crippled boy,' I was disappointed and deeply hurt.

"One day my mother and I went to visit our grand-aunt in the neighborhood. My grand-aunt was my favorite relative because she had always been so kind to me. When we arrived, my grand-aunt gave me a stalk of sugarcane to eat. I was delighted and thanked her for her generosity and immediately went outside to eat my sugarcane. As I had not tasted candy for a long time, I began to eat slowly, savoring every bite of it.

"Suddenly I noted that a pair of small eyes were staring at my sugarcane--a small boy from the neighborhood was watching my candy like a cat watching a bird. I started to leave, but he begged, 'Can I share a small bite, Big Brother?' I looked at my piece of sugarcane for a moment and then looked at the boy, and found him rather pitiable and sincere, and probably like myself having been without candy for a long time. I looked at my delicious candy again and finally decided that I would share one tiny bite with this innocent boy. The instant I handed him the sugarcane, he ran off! On the brink of losing my candy, I chased after him. However, as soon as I took my first step, I fell. I got up and ran, and fell again. Helplessly I watched him disappear into the street.

"After a few such discouraging experiences, I began to feel inferior to the other boys. But my mother encouraged me and gave me pride, 'My son, you are a capable young man. You have a sound mind and you will have a good future.' Even though I believed in her, reality was not at all good to me. As I grew older I needed to earn a living for myself. In an attempt to find a place to work, I went to all the merchants in town and said, 'Sir. I am a capable man and I am willing to work for food.' However, the answer was always no. They never stated directly that it was because I was a cripple, and always found other reasons to refuse me. But I knew better.

"One day a shopkeeper said to me, 'Our shop owner has left town and I have temporarily taken over his place. If you are willing to work for food you can start tomorrow!' These were the sweetest words I had heard in a long time, and I became the happiest man in the whole world.

"Early next morning I put on my best clothes and started to work as the shopkeeper's assistant. I greeted people with smiles and helped clean the stalls. I also arranged merchandise, swept floors, and served meals to all the shopkeepers and their assistants. I worked very hard and wanted to please everybody. After each day's work the shopkeeper gave me a large bowl of rice to bring home.

'Young man, work harder and I will ask our owner to give you a raise when he comes back.' The shopkeeper always encouraged me whenever he gave me the rice for the day.

"Wanting to please my mother by gaining a raise, I worked harder and longer each day. One day I heard that the shop owner had come back and I was looking forward to a raise. At the end of the day I came to the shopkeeper as usual, taking the bowl of rice, and expecting to hear the good news.

'I am sorry to tell you that you are no longer needed here.' Shocked, I didn't know what to do when the shopkeeper broke the news to me.

'Why?' I asked.

'The owner said that the sight of a cripple will drive away business.'

"I started to get angry but by now life had taught me the harsh reality of being crippled. Instead of arguing with him, I begged, 'Please, sir, tell the owner that I will work for food only and I will stay out of sight!'

'Sorry, young man, I already did my best.'

"Having received my last bowl of rice, I took the longest way home.

"Again I had hoped to find a job but nobody seemed to be interested. I became gloomy and melancholy and gradually I became crippled inside.

"One day my mother said to me, 'My son, when the horse dies you walk. I have found you a job as a water buffalo tender.'

"Buffalo tending was the lowest type of work, usually reserved for the old and the very weak. However, my mind was so bruised by the cruel reality of being crippled that I was willing to do anything to sustain my miserable life.

"So I became a buffalo tender. I was now at the prime marrying age and my mother was trying to find me a wife. Though she understood that there was little hope for a buffalo tender to find a wife, still she tried. In our neighborhood, there was an ugly old maid who had never had any young men propose to her. My mother thought I would be better off by marrying an old maid than not marrying at all.

"At first I refused to go along with this, but my mother insisted that

it was my responsibility to carry on our family name, so I finally
agreed. My mother acted immediately and asked me to wait outside
our house. I saw her go into the old maid's house and soon I heard loud
curses coming from inside the house. Then I saw my mother being
chased out by the old maid's mother. 'A crippled buffalo tender trying
to marry my daughter? An ugly toad wants to eat the heavenly goose
meat?' She said this so loudly that the whole neighborhood heard her
words.

"I was so embarrassed that I quickly hobbled into the fields to find
comfort with my buffalos. From that day onward, I totally withdrew
from people and seldom smiled--I had lost my confidence in humanity.
My buffalos became my daily companions and I learned how to play
the bamboo flute which gave me some comfort.

"One beautiful spring day, I was alone on the hillside overlooking
a rainbow which arched down to the horizon. I could see our village
in the distance. Blue jays, sparrows, finches, and woodpeckers were
busy celebrating the spring. Plum flowers, peach flowers, dogwood
flowers and all the beautiful spring flowers were blossoming
everywhere. The water buffalos were gently grazing in the tender
grass. Everything was in perfect harmony. Feeling that I was the only
sad creature in this perfect spring day, I took out the bamboo flute and
played a song:

> "White clouds are floating high in the sky beyond the Yellow
> River.
> Among the endless mountains there is a lonely city;
> Bamboo Flute, why do you blame the willows,
> When you know that spring wind doesn't pass the Yunmon
> Gate?

"The song reminded me that there would be no more springs for
me and I felt pity for myself and sobbed.

'Why are you crying, my child?' a kind voice asked me. I looked
up and saw a holy man sitting on a rock.

"I did not answer and he continued, 'It was a beautiful song you
were playing. Once I knew that song well because I felt the same way
you do. How old are you, my child?' His voice was kind and concerned.

'I am nineteen years old, sir,' I replied.

'Why do you feel that spring will not come to you at your young age?' benignly, he asked.

'I am crippled, sir.' My eyes looked down to the ground.

'Have you tried to bring spring to yourself?'

'Yes, I have tried everything; and so has my mother,' I replied sadly, shaking my head.

'If I tell you there is a divine plan in which everybody is born to be useful, would you believe me?'

'No,' I replied because I did not believe I was useful.

'Are the water buffalos useful for farmers?' Unimpressed by my pessimism, he continued to ask.

'Yes, they are essential for the cultivation of the farmland.' I was proud of my buffalos.

'Are you tending the buffalos so that they can be strong and help the farmers?'

'The buffalos I am tending are the strongest in the village,' I replied proudly, pointing to my cattle.

'So you are doing a useful job for the village by tending the buffalos, aren't you?'

"He led me to believe that I was useful. Yet, I had never thought being a buffalo tender was very useful, so I replied, 'If the divine plan for me is to be a useful buffalo tender, I would rather not have been born.'

'Come over here, my child,' asked the holy man and waved me to his side. 'Look at these ants.' He pointed to some ants which were busy gathering food and commented, 'Even ants want to live. It is a wonderful world, my child.'

'I wish I were as simple as the ants, sir. But I have a mind that troubles me.'

'How?'

'Sometimes when I see the birds so happy I become happy. But as soon as I feel happy there is something in my memory, telling me that I could have been happier if I had had two legs. Then I feel hopeless because I have nothing to look forward to in my life. I am afraid I cannot support myself when I get old.'

'My child, I understand that you had many good days before you lost your leg and you have had bad days ever since; and you are worrying about your future, and thus conclude that your whole life is bad. But, my child, why do you sum up your life's worth while you are still in the game of life?

'We cannot predict what tomorrow will bring. Look at the sun, my child.' He pointed to the midday sun and continued, 'Under the sun we are all equal. You are the child of the universe, and you have as much right as anybody else to live here, to breathe freely, to express your feelings, to be proud, to have dignity and most of all, to be yourself. Before this sun goes down today, and every day from now on, make a promise to yourself to be yourself today, not yesterday or tomorrow. Live one day at a time and live it fully. Remember that the future is not for us to see. Everything happens for a reason and your misfortune may be a blessing in disguise. Do you remember these writings?

'Whenever life is on your way you should enjoy it fully.

Don't wait until the golden bottle becomes dry then watch the empty moon.

Heaven has given life to you therefore you are useful.

Today you have lost all your treasures but tomorrow they will be returned.'

"I nodded but asked, 'I have lost my leg, can Heaven give it back to me?'

'Yes, it will, my child. However, it will not be in the form of a leg but it will be in other forms.'

'How do you know, holy man?'

'I have been there, my child, I have been there. My life has treated me even worse than you were treated. Yet, the valuables I have lost have since returned to me many times. So believe in yourself and know that you are heavenly born to be useful. Live one day at a time and have faith that every tragedy is a blessing in disguise, for everything happens with a purpose.' After saying that he started to walk away.

"Suddenly I saw that he was walking on his *hands*, not his feet. Both of his legs were crippled. I rushed to follow him but he had disappeared like the wind.

"After seeing this crippled holy man, I felt lucky because I could still walk with one good leg. I told myself that if this holy man could survive I could too. Each morning when I woke up, I asked myself, 'Everything happens with a purpose, how do I know my present sufferings are not my future blessings?' My mind had freed itself from worrying about my future and I began to appreciate things around me. As a result, I felt happy again and started to enjoy my job as a buffalo tender.

"With the belief that if I were heavenly born to be a buffalo tender I might as well be the best one on earth, I began to pay attention to my buffalos and studied their habits. By gaining more knowledge about the buffalos, I started experiments in breeding high quality calves. Soon I became a well-known breeder and people from far away came to me for calves. I was building up a thriving buffalo breeding business until an unexpected event happened which changed my life again.

"One day a group of soldiers came and rounded up all the able males, both young and old, and forced them to fight the invading barbarians. I was spared because of my broken leg. One month later news came that all the drafted men from our region were ambushed by the enemy and no one had escaped.

"Suddenly I became the only able male in the entire region! I soon found myself the center of attention. I received hundreds of proposals for marriage and each offered land and money as wedding gifts. The offers became greater and greater as time went by, once the women were sure their men would not be back. Some of the widows became so desperate that they offered to mate with me so that they could have heirs!

"Not wanting to mate like the buffalos, I refused their offers. Yet, they kept on coming and finally I decided to choose the most beautiful maidens in this area and married them. Because they brought me much land and money, I was able to take many beautiful brides. Consequently, I fathered many children and many of them inherited their mothers' beauty, which led our village to become known as the Village of Beauties.' Mr. Old Cripple smiled.

Zhang Yang

Suddenly I saw that he was walking on his hands, not his feet. Both of his legs were crippled. I rushed to follow him but he had disappeared like the wind.

"What happened to the boy who ran away with your candy and the shop owner who dismissed you?" I asked.

"They were killed in the ambush, I am sure."

"And what happened to the old maid who refused to marry you?"

"She became much happier after the tragedy."

"Did you mate with her?" I whispered.

"Absolutely not!" he raised his voice, still showing emotion toward his spurned love after all those years.

"Why did she become happier?" I was curious.

"She was no longer the only old maid in the village!" he brushed his white beard and laughed heartily.

I thanked Mr. Old Cripple and bade him good night. After a few days' rest, I was on my way back to Grandmaster and Lotus.

Lotus was waiting for me where we had parted. We were extremely happy to see each other. I told her all about my journey, then Lotus said she was to have a poetry final examination tomorrow but was not prepared because she had been thinking about me.

Next morning I waited anxiously outside her classroom for her to finish the examination so we could take a horse ride together. Suddenly I heard the teacher shouting, "Get out! You, get out!" After a while, Lotus emerged from the classroom, her face red and her body trembling with embarrassment.

"What's wrong, Lotus?" I asked.

She looked down at the path and did not reply.

"Have you completed your examination? Please tell me. I care about you."

She finally said, "My teacher tore up my answer sheets."

"What did you do?"

"I don't know exactly. But when I received the questions, I panicked. One of the questions asked us to write down a long poem and I went blank. All I needed was a hint in order to remember the whole poem. Without knowing why, I felt the compulsion to look over the shoulders of the girl in front of me. Our teacher saw me do this and expelled me."

"You were cheating. You shouldn't have done that, Lotus." I

patronized her.

"But I don't know why I did it. It happened so quickly that my act was totally out of my control. It seemed at the moment I was somebody else. I feel terribly embarrassed now and I need a place to hide away. You are the only one who cares." She was trying to find comfort from me.

Instead of comforting her, I lectured her, "But, Lotus, cheating is cheating, and cheating is dishonest. You should feel ashamed."

Lotus was shocked by my remark and ran away to the Reflecting Pond with her hands covering her face. I followed her and found her, curled up in one corner, filled with guilt.

I wanted to come close to her and comfort her, but I was afraid my words would hurt her even more. So I sat on the grass, trying to understand her plight by putting myself into her position. I remembered when I was in school I had done the same thing--I looked over a classmate's shoulder during a language examination because I had forgotten the examination date and had not prepared for it. Even though my teacher did not discover my cheating, I was afraid to look her in the eye. I always felt she knew, and was ashamed.

Why did I perform such a dishonorable act? Maybe I was temporarily insane? Now that I admitted I might temporarily not be myself during some moments of my life, I recalled many other incidents during which I could not explain why I had acted the way I did, other than I was not fully functioning when it all happened.

On one occasion I met a girl for the first time and mistakenly thought she had fallen in love with me. So I wrote her a love letter as though we were already lovers. The girl showed the letter to her parents who protested loudly and embarrassed my whole family in front of others. I became so intimidated that I never talked to that girl again. My mother told me that she understood these things often happen and advised me to forget this episode. But I was a model son and could not believe I had acted so foolishly. I couldn't reconcile my irrational deeds with my rational mind, so I suppressed these memories as soon as they came into focus. Indeed, love provokes strong emotions and strong emotions make big fools of us.

The Reflecting Pond was unusually calm and the sky was incredibly blue today. I got up, bent over and looked at my own image in the pond. Suddenly I felt as if it were speaking to me, "Why are you so harsh toward Lotus when you yourself have done the same irrational deeds? Hasn't she suffered enough for her act? Forgive her, forgive her."

"I don't know how to forgive her."

"If you truly love her, you will forgive her."

"It is not that I don't love her; but I have carried the same thorns all my life. How can I truly forgive her if I have not forgiven myself?"

"Can't you pluck those thorns out of your memory?"

"How?" I shook my head and looked beyond the pond. In the distant fields, there were some water buffalos grazing peacefully on the horizon. Suddenly I thought of Mr. Old Cripple and I looked down at my reflection again and asked, "Why should I pluck out my thorns when they might be blessings in disguise? Perhaps these thorns are just as useful as the thorns protecting the beautiful roses?"

"What then should you do?"

"I should love them all, both thorns and roses. Yet, just as we look at roses we concentrate on their beautiful petals and not their thorns; when we look at our lives we concentrate on our blessings not our misgivings. Besides, aren't roses and thorns, blessings and misgivings examples of yin and yang, necessary for each other's existence?"

Then I remembered there was still one rose remaining in the rose garden. I ran to the garden to pick the rose for Lotus but it was gone.

"Looking for thorns?" someone asked. I turned around and found it was Lotus.

"No, I am looking for roses," I answered.

"Here," Lotus handed me a beautiful red rose. "But it comes with thorns," she warned.

"They only make me treat my precious rose with much tender loving care," I replied as she gave me the red rose.

As soon as I held the rose in my hand, I developed a wonderful feeling about it and took a deep breath, filling my body with its sweet fragrance. Meanwhile Grandmaster called for Lotus and she left.

With the red rose still in my hand, I went to the Reflecting Pond alone. The pond surface had turned into a smooth mirror as it had done countless times before. Standing there alone, I was admiring the timelessness of this natural pond, for it was still proudly being itself while all its admirers had come and gone. As I looked deeply into the pond, I realized that it, too, was admiring me for my brief joyful moment on this earth with freedom to move and act on my dreams. When I looked at the beautiful rose in my hand again, it seemed to become bigger and brighter until it had turned into a large red lantern, illuminating my mind. I felt delighted and joy rushed through my body as I realized that this beautiful red rose itself, with its thorns symbolizing the yin, the sorrowful part of our lives, and its petals symbolizing the yang, the joyful part of our lives, was indeed, the Fifth Secret of the Tai Chi Circle.

Now I was more resolved to follow my dreams because failures did not frighten me anymore. For if I have acted on my dreams and failed, people may laugh at me, humiliate me, look down on me, even step on me; but after all, how can they be so sure that my failures are not my successes in disguise?

These words had finally found a place in my heart and they resonated through my soul:

Everything happens with a purpose; this, too, might be a blessing in disguise.

Everything happens with a purpose; this, too, might be a blessing in disguise.

Everything happens with a purpose; this, too, might be a blessing in disguise.

Chapter Seven

Rainbow

Today was the Lunar July Seventh Festival. Grandmaster told me there would be no Tai Chi lesson given during the day but that the lesson would be held tonight at the Reflecting Pond.

I was looking forward to the special lesson tonight and arrived at the Reflecting Pond early. I was alone, watching the sun go down in the distant mountains. The serenity of the environment reminded me of this poem:

> Somewhere amid the pine trees lies a temple;
> Faintly I hear the sound of the evening bell in the distance.
> Wearing a straw hat I carry my long shadow in the twilight;
> Toward the faraway green mountains I walk alone.

Night had fallen and nature's sounds abounded. Then I became aware that Grandmaster was already here.

"Look at the stars, Yee. Can you find the North Star?"

Looking at the sky, I found it already filled with stars. I traced the seven bright stars to the North Star, which was directly above the mountains, and told Grandmaster that I had found it.

"Yee, can you locate the Buffalo Boy Star and the Weaver Lady Star?"

I did not know where to begin and so I asked, "Grandmaster, I cannot locate them. Can you help me? And why are people celebrating these two stars tonight?"

"People celebrate these stars tonight because, on this night, true lovers are united. According to legend a fairy once visited the earth and fell in love with a handsome young buffalo boy. The buffalo boy did not know that his beautiful wife was from Heaven. They married and soon they had two sons and lived happily as a family. When the head fairy found out that one of her fairies had settled down on the earth as a weaver, she ordered her to come back to Heaven at once. Reluctantly the wife ascended to Heaven. When she arrived she was locked into one of the brightest stars in Heaven. When the buffalo boy found out that his wife had flown to the stars, he carried his two sons and followed her to the end of the earth. The head fairy took pity on this true lover and assigned to him another bright star. However, these two lovers are separated by millions of stars in the Silver River. Only once a year, on July the seventh, the stars become birds to form a bridge enabling them to walk across the Silver River to meet each other.

"Yee, look at the lower side of the Silver River," suggested Grandmaster, pointing to the sky. "The brighter star, with two dim stars equally spaced on either side of it, is called the Buffalo Boy Star. The two dim stars are his sons." Then he pointed to a star across the Silver River opposite from the Buffalo Boy Star and said, "This brighter star is the Weaver Lady Star. Can you find them?"

"Yes, Grandmaster." I was excited since I could identify the stars, and they all seemed to becoming alive.

"But Grandmaster, do you believe the story?"

"This is only folklore, which humanizes the stars so that we can identify with them. Let us look at the ocean of stars for a while, perhaps they may inspire us tonight." Grandmaster signaled me to be quiet.

In front of these endless, faraway stars, I felt very small and humble. My mind pondered: What worlds are there floating in the twinkling night sky? Are there creatures like ourselves staring into the same universe tonight and wondering the same thing? Is the ocean of stars the theater of the universe for all living beings to stare at and wonder about?

"Grandmaster, are there people in all the stars out there?" I broke the silence.

"It is beyond my knowledge, Yee. However, I do know that there are stars in all people."

"What do you mean, Grandmaster?"

"Our body has a network of meridians through which life energy, Chi, flows just as there is a network of blood vessels through which blood flows. There are many energy points at fixed locations along the meridians and they scatter within our body like star clusters. These meridians exist at all times within a living person but they disappear when a person dies. Our ancestors discovered this mysterious network of meridians through generations of human experience and have made use of them for keeping our bodies healthy; in like fashion, they discovered the mysterious energy field which makes iron point to the North and have made use of it for finding the directions. And just as the stars only reveal themselves to us on cloudless nights, so the energy stars in our body reveal themselves only when our minds are clear."

"How can we make our minds clear so that we can feel the energy points in our body, Grandmaster?"

"The Tai Chi way of obtaining a clear mind is through movement. Instead of focusing our mind on one particular point or nothing at all, we move our mind from one energy point to another continuously whenever we execute Tai Chi movements. You can feel the life energy go through your energy points when you are relaxed and calm. The Tai Chi exercise is slow because it takes time to move our mind from one point to another. If you move too quickly you will not be able to direct your life energy through your body and you will lose your concentration."

"Grandmaster, are the energy points the same as those recognized in medicine?"

"Yes, doctors use the same system to cure their patients. They know that our body contains a network of energy points and that life energy flows through them. If blockages occur between energy points, they will affect the balance of our body and cause illness. To treat patients, traditional doctors use herbal medicine to unclog these blockages; whereas the acupuncturists use needles to stimulate their patients' energy points to restore their energy balance. Since in Tai Chi exercises we stimulate our energy points by thinking about them, we keep our life energy flowing freely and vigorously through our systems. As a result we prevent illness and keep our lives in a state of vigorous health, not merely in an absence of illness. The key is to exercise often, Yee," Grandmaster explained.

"Why is exercise so important in keeping us healthy, Grandmaster?"

"Each time we exercise, we keep our life energy, Chi, and blood flowing through our body unblocked. As a result, our bodies remain healthy. What if we don't exercise at all? There was an ancient story about a lazy lady who never did anything and relied totally on her husband. One time her husband had to leave home for a few days on an important trip. Before he left, he fixed a huge rice biscuit and hung it from his wife's neck to make sure she would not be hungry. When he came back, he was dismayed to have found his wife had died. Then he discovered that his wife had eaten only the portion of the biscuit hanging closest to her.

"Did hunger alone kill the lady? It was unlikely because a healthy person could have survived a few days without food. It was the lack of exercise that had killed her, for her life energy and blood had been gradually blocked up through the years when she remained idle. Without life energy, how could she remain alive?"

"Grandmaster, if we can just do some exercise to keep our bodies healthy, why do we place such emphasis on clearing our mind?"

"Yee, the health of our body is greatly affected by our mind. The mind can keep our life energy flowing freely in our body. However, the mind can also do the opposite. If it is our mind that blocks our life energy, only our mind can unblock it. Physical exercise and medicine alone will not help us to solve the blockages created by our mind.

"How does our mind affect our health? Let me tell you a story about a couple who had been living happily for many years. One night, the husband had a dream that the sky was going to collapse and that he would be killed. When he woke up, he was afraid, but he decided not to tell his beloved wife so that she could continue her happy life.

"From that day onward, the husband could not eat during the day and could not sleep at night. His hair started to fall out and his body lost weight. His wife was concerned and invited all the famous doctors in the area to cure his illness. But none of the doctors could find anything wrong with her husband and they all told her that he was just exhausted from working.

"Then one night the wife found out the truth about her husband's illness when he spoke aloud in his dreams. The next day, she told him that the sky was made of air just like the air around him, and therefore, even if it fell, it would not squash him.

'How about the moon, the sun, and the stars?' her husband asked, still unconvinced.

'They are also nothing but hot air. If they collapse on you, the air will become cool and it won't hurt you,' replied the wife.

"Like getting 'a big stone off his chest,' the man was now able to eat and sleep again. The couple returned to their normal lives and they lived happily ever after.

"Yee, as you see, the mind affects our health and often only the mind can solve the problems created by itself." Grandmaster finished talking and we remained quiet.

I stared at the stars and realized that the ocean of stars in the night sky was truly miraculous. Then when I thought of the stars inside my body, I realized I was a miracle too, even though on a lesser scale. A thought came to my mind and I asked, "Grandmaster, if our body resembles the universe and we are living beings, isn't the universe also a living being?"

"Indeed, we are a part of living nature and we closely resemble things around us. For instance, a female adult takes the same number of days to complete her womanly cycle as does a new moon to become a waning moon; and it takes her nine such cycles for childbearing. Our feelings are also related to nature: We feel lively when we see new leaves sprouting during the spring and feel nostalgic when we see the old leaves falling down in autumn. Since we are a part of nature, we feel happy when we return to it, just like a bird is happy when it is freed from a cage. Now, let's close our eyes and listen to the sounds of nature."

I closed my eyes and I heard the wind blowing, the crickets chirping, night birds crying, and animals howling.

"Do you hear the crickets?" Grandmaster asked.

"Yes, a lot of them. They all seem to vibrate in the same monotonous, chaotic way," I answered.

"Now, calm your mind by repeating to yourself 'all creatures are quiet,'" Grandmaster suggested softly.

As I repeated the sentence over and over again, I found my mind had become quiet while all the creatures around me were making sounds, as if they were celebrating life. The chaotic sounds had suddenly become the orderly sounds of individual crickets. Indeed, I had blended into mother nature and I felt very, very happy.

"Grandmaster, I have found that there are patterns to the sounds of nature. They are very interesting and pleasant. Why didn't I notice this before?"

"Yee, you can find order and harmony in all things if you have a serene mind. When your mind is cluttered with unnecessary thoughts, you will find it easier to dismiss something as out of order than to find out the actual order of something."

"Grandmaster, do you mean we should always look for harmony in nature, including in people?"

"Aren't people also a part of nature? We cannot find harmony in people if we walk the easy way: It is easier to find fault in others than it is to find virtues because all of us have many faults. It is easier to criticize what people have done than to appreciate their accomplishments because things are easier said than done."

"So when we come to the wilderness as we have done tonight, we can learn the lesson of harmony so that we can live harmoniously with other people?"

"Yes, we are social creatures and we depend on each other for survival. However, we have built an artificial world which has shielded us from the real one. Why do we feel happy when we are with the stars, the rivers, the mountains, and other creatures?" Grandmaster paused and continued, "Because we are part of living nature and we need to return to it from time to time to regain a proper perspective."

Grandmaster finished tonight's lesson and we camped out in the open, near the Reflecting Pond.

Soon I found myself in a dream. I was standing on a mountaintop above a lake in the middle of winter. I was following Grandmaster's suggestion to look for patterns of beauty in nature. But I could not find anything interesting. There were no chirping of insects or howling of animals, only bare trees standing silently against the cold wind. Just as I dismissed the weather as miserable, an ancient poet suddenly made his appearance and greeted me, "It is a beautiful day, isn't it?"

"I can't find the beauty in it, Mr. Poet," I replied.

"Haven't you seen the small boat in the middle of the lake?"

"Yes, now that you mention it," I answered and instantly recalled this poem:

> A thousand mountains have all the birds flown away.
> Ten thousand tracks are without human footprints;
> Yet there is a solitary boat with an old man in thick straw clothes,
> Snow fishing in the frigid river alone.

I now began to recognize the beauty of winter in this tranquil environment, which reflected the serenity within myself. I felt delighted and asked, "How do you famous poets enjoy the seasons?"

The Poet replied, "We celebrate the seasons. We poets understand that each season has its own beauty even though beauty is sometimes concealed by harshness. We have developed the habit of looking for the wonderful things each season brings to us."

"Can you show me how?"

"I will show you how. Now come and fly with me." He held my hand and together we flew into the air effortlessly!

"Where are you taking me, Mr. Poet?"

"I am leading you to a place where there is summertime."

Soon we landed in a place where the air was hot and sultry. I sweated and felt the oppressiveness of the heat immediately. Instead of enjoying the sunshine, I began to complain.

"Why are you fighting the heat?" the Poet asked. "Accept it and look for the beauty which is to be found in these lovely summer days! The summer won't last forever and you had better enjoy it while it lasts."

I followed his advice and turned my mind to the joy and fun of the summer days. Strangely the heat seemed to become bearable as I looked for beautiful things on this sunny day. I felt refreshed and cool, and remembered this poem:

> Green trees form cool shadows during the long summer days.
> The decorated balcony reflects in the perfectly still pond;
> Crystal curtain moves as the summer breeze begins.
> Fragrance of the honeysuckle fills the garden air.

"Come fly with me into spring." The Poet held my hand and soon we were in the air again.

As we were flying, I recalled this poem:

> Letting each day pass away in a tipsy dreamy way,
> I heard the spring would soon be past I climbed the mountain fast;
> Listening to a holy man in a bamboo temple by chance,
> I glimpsed a moment of peace in this floating life hence.

I asked the Poet the meaning of this poem. He told me that our lives were made up of seasons and that most people neglected the seasons until it was too late.

"Mr. Poet, why can't most of us appreciate the joy of each season?"

"Because most people are so preoccupied with their past and their future that they forget to celebrate the present. They have built their own worlds in which there are no seasons," the Poet answered. Then he held my hand tightly and said, "Come, before your seasons are over, come, fly with me to the joy of seasons!"

Soon we reached a spot where flowers were blossoming and birds were singing. I had thought spring was a perfect time of the year and people should be happy, but then came the rain. People began to run for shelter and many of them complained about the rain which had interrupted their activities. However, there was one man happily dancing in the rain! I looked closely and recognized that he was the famous poet, Li Bai, who was singing his own famous poem:

> "Sweep Tomb period is the time of rain.
> Travelers on the road almost lose their soul.
> May I ask where can I find a place to have a treat?
> The buffalo boy points to the faraway Apricot Flowers Street."

Then the rain stopped and people resumed their routine activities. I noticed a spider, whose body was covered with tiny raindrops, behaving strangely, moving rapidly from one end of its web to another for no apparent reason.

"Look, Mr. Poet. I have found a spider who is going berserk!" I shouted excitedly, pointing to the tiny creature.

He smiled and said, "This is a world of wonders and 'ten thousand

Come, before your seasons are over, come, fly with me to the joy of seasons!

things being observed in serenity' will reveal their beauties to you."

I followed his advice and observed the spider quietly. Soon I found the spider moving in some kind of pattern. Perhaps it was trying to shake the rain drops off its body and web? Or perhaps it was trying to attract its prey by creating some motion? It was clear to me that the spider was following some instinct essential for its survival. Was there anything in common between this particular spider and me? I wondered and touched its body with a leaf. The spider quickly withdrew and disappeared into the bushes. Yes--survival! Both the spider and I wanted to live, hang on to life as long as possible.

I pondered: Isn't it true that the common desire among all living things is to live? If being alive is a wonderful thing, do I sometimes wonder how a spider, a bee, a beaver, a squirrel, or a butterfly makes it in this world? Or do I care? If I do care, isn't it wonderful to observe how other living creatures strive to survive? And in turn, don't these creatures remind us to care more about our own human survival in this wonderful world? Indeed, if one observes things with a serene mind, one can find that we are not alone in this palace of wonders.

As I meditated on these things, the Poet held my hand and whispered, "Let's travel to autumn." And up we flew into the air.

Soon we flew over many houses and saw some people raking leaves. Hearing many of them complain that there were more leaves this year than last, the Poet smiled and shook his head. We continued to fly until we reached the top of a mountain, overlooking a colorful autumn forest. This poem of autumn came to my mind:

> A clear brook flows through a beautiful mountaintop;
> Blue sky and clean water reflect the autumn colors.
> I am separated from the rest of the world in thirty Li;
> White clouds and red leaves are my only companions.

Wanting to fly down to the trees to fetch some of the leaves, I glided downward. However, I suddenly awakened with a start and found that I had almost fallen into the Reflecting Pond! It was morning and Grandmaster had already gone when I woke up from my dream. Quickly I got up and went directly to Grandmaster and told him about my dream.

After I finished telling him I asked, "Grandmaster, the Poet talked about serenity and so did you. Why do people want to achieve the state of being serene?"

"Because people want to achieve amazing things."

"What do you mean, Grandmaster?"

"When the observer and the observed have become one, the secrets of the observed will reveal themselves to the observer. For example, look at this bonsai," said Grandmaster, pointing to a beautiful dwarfed pine tree in a small pot. "When a mediocre painter sees the bonsai, he will be thinking about its colors, its lines, its background, and how to blend them together to form a beautiful picture. But such a painting, no matter how closely it resembles the real tree, can only reflect the mind of the observer, not the true beauty of the observed. On the other hand, when a master painter sees such a bonsai, he observes the tree in serenity, forgets about his intention to paint, and becomes the tree itself. When this happens, he captures the spirit of the tree and his painting will show the true beauty of the bonsai and become a masterpiece."

"Grandmaster, what if the observer is not a painter, will the bonsai tree still have secrets for him?"

"When you have a serene mind, the tree becomes you, and you the tree. It will reveal its secrets to you depending upon what you want from it. When a mediocre merchant sees the pine tree, he probably will begin calculating the cost of raising the tree, the cost of its container, transportation, and his profits. But when a great merchant sees it, instead of making a judgment about the thing he is watching, he observes the bonsai with serenity; when he and the tree have become one, the tree will reveal to him the most important information about his trade: Will there be a market for it? His intuition seldom fails him and he remains at the top of his field."

"Grandmaster, I remember you have taught me the art of selling by forgetting myself. Are you now teaching me the same thing here?"

"Yes, the same principle applies here except you are dealing with different subjects here. Before, we were talking about the relationship of people to people, just as in the Tai Chi Push Hands exercise--you and your opponent. Now we are talking about the relationship of people to things, just as in the Tai Chi exercise--you and the Tai Chi movements."

After thanking Grandmaster for his teaching, I went back to the Reflecting Pond to meet Lotus. While I was waiting, I discovered a spider in its web among the bush. I observed the creature in silence until a voice startled me, "Watching mosses grow, ah?" Lotus smiled.

"Last night I had a dream in which I met an ancient poet."

"Really? What happened?"

After I told her my dream, Lotus said, "That reminds me of a story about poets: a good poet and a mediocre poet."

"Can you tell me about it?"

Lotus told the following story: "Once there was a poet who wanted to see who was a better scholar, his nephew or his niece. So he articulated a sentence and asked each of them to match it.

"After a moment the nephew replied:

'Snow falling in the air what can be so fair?

Throwing salts into the air can hardly compare!'

"Then the niece came up with hers:

'Snow falling in the air what can be so fair?

Not as fair as the catkin seeds floating in the air!'

"I guess the niece's was better?" I asked.

"Can't you see that the man thought only of mundane salt whereas the lady appreciated the beauty of nature?"

It sounded like a challenge for me to come up with an interesting poem. Luckily I found one and asked her, "Do you remember the poem by a lazy poet who did not want to study?"

"No, tell me."

I recited:

"Spring seasons are not studying reasons.

Summer is hot therefore it is good for a cot;

Wait till fall and winter will soon call.

I better close my bag until next year's back."

As Lotus laughed, I noticed that she was wearing a funny looking hat with a large rim and with a tall funnel-shaped head in the middle. She handed me a similar hat and told me that it was a gift from Great-

Grandmaster, who had just come back from his current travels. He had told her that these hats were souvenirs obtained from a tribe of mountain people. We should treasure these hats because they were very beautiful and were used by the local lovers in their courtships.

Beautiful? For courtship? We laughed loudly when we looked at the hats. The more we teased about the hats the funnier they looked. Soon we started to toss the hats around, treating them as fun toys. As we threw the hats at each other, Lotus stepped on hers and broke its head. It looked even more bizarre with its head dangling from the rest of the hat.

We could hardly stop laughing at our new toys. Like a kite, the broken hat lingered in the air as I threw it high into the sky. The wind blew it farther away, and it fell down in front of Great-Grandmaster, who was taking a walk nearby. He picked up the damaged gift, pressed it to his heart and left without saying a word. Lotus immediately followed to comfort him, leaving me alone with my hat.

Why did Great-Grandmaster treat such a simple hat with so much respect? While I looked at my hat, I remembered that Grandmaster had told me that I should use the very same serene approach in my understanding of the beauty of the Tai Chi movements, to find beauty in things. I had not done so and I felt embarrassed. Facing the calm pond, I sheepishly put on the hat and practiced my Tai Chi movements.

As I breathed in deeply and breathed out slowly and evenly, my mind became serene and clear. Gradually, I felt I was floating among clouds and my movements were flowing as continuously as water flowing in the river. Indeed, I had become the very movements themselves.

When I finished my Tai Chi exercise, I looked at the pond where the water was calm and clear. Then I looked beyond the pond and noticed for the first time a strangely shaped mountain far, far away. Its shape seemed very familiar, as though I had seen it somewhere before. Inadvertently I looked down at the water and saw my own image along with that of my hat reflected in the pond--the shape of the hat matched perfectly that of the mountain!

Then it dawned on me that the area from which the hat originated was famous for this beautiful mountain. Indeed, the natives had recognized the beauty of such a shape and had achieved harmony with the mountains by creating objects with analogous shapes. The young had learned from their elders to appreciate the beauty of nature, and had used its contour as a symbol of beauty and love.

Now with a serene mind, I could appreciate the beauty of the hat instead of dismissing it as without beauty merely because it looked so different from anything I was accustomed to. When I looked at the other side of the pond, I saw my beloved Lotus standing in the distance wearing her beautiful hat, a perfect match with the distant mountain.

For a brief moment, everything around the pond seemed to have remained quiet. The insects, birds, animals, and all creatures were quiet. Then a rainbow appeared in the distant sky as the sunlight penetrated the moist air. With much admiration, I uttered, "Oh, it is such a wonderful world!" As I listened to the silence, I closed my eyes and felt my heart beating, my breathing, and life energy flowing through my body. I realized the world inside myself was just as miraculous as the one outside myself. With the same admiration, I uttered from the depth of my heart,"Oh, what a miraculous world I have inside myself! What a miracle I am!"

While I remained quiet and breathed deeply, I realized the barrier between my yin, inner world, and the yang, outside world had disappeared, forming a perfect Tai Chi Circle, connecting me to the unlimited supply of energy in the universe. The moment when nature and I had become one, I had such a wonderful feeling about being alive that it was beyond description. I could only communicate how I felt with a smile. Such a wonderful feeling, indeed, was the Sixth Secret of the Tai Chi Circle! These words were appearing in my mind again and again to remind me to love nature:

Fly to the joy of seasons, be with the mountains, the rivers, the stars, and all the living things, for this is a wonderful world.

Fly to the joy of seasons, be with the mountains, the rivers, the stars, and all the living things, for this is a wonderful world.

Fly to the joy of seasons, be with the mountains, the rivers, the stars, and all the living things, for this is a wonderful world.

Chapter Eight

Flower

Great-Great-Grandmaster died one day while he was peacefully sleeping in his bed. Everyone in the village showed up to pay their last respects to this inspiring gentleman. After they buried his body in his beloved mountains, I went to the Reflecting Pond alone. His death reminded me of home and my mother's vulnerability, for she too was getting old. I still vividly remembered the poem she had quoted when she bade me goodbye:

> Seeing you off among these mountains,
> At twilight I close the wooden door alone.
> When the spring grass turns green next year,
> Will the traveler be returning home then?

The grass had turned green five times since I left home. Why had I never thought much of my mother until now? It was not that I did not care about her, but I had taken it for granted that both of us would be healthy when I came back to her one day.

Then I remembered my relationship with my father when I was growing up. When I was young, my father often forgot I was only a child and used his own standards in finding fault with me. When I played games with other children, he would drag me home and force me to study. One time when I proudly showed him the flower chain I had made, he punished me because he thought the flowers should have remained in the garden. I knew my father loved me, but he never tried to understand why I did such silly childish things. Indeed, he had viewed me as an adult and had expected too much from me. Yet, I never resented him and always felt a spontaneous childlike love for him.

One day my father became sick and was impatient with me. He could not wait for his bowl of herbal medicine to cool down before shouting for me to carry it to him. I ran into the kitchen and carried the medicine to him. The bowl was extremely hot but I ignored it because I wanted my father to get well soon. When he took the bowl, he immediately put it down on the table as the bowl scorched him. He looked at me and asked me to show him my hands--they were as red as a hot iron. My father embraced me for the first time in my life and murmured to himself, "Oh, for Heaven's sake, he is only a child. He is only a child."

I always thought of my father as young, even though he was quite old when he married my mother. When I became a young adult I never had time for him as I was too busy with my own studies, friends, and daily routine. One day he died of old age and it was then too late for me to make up for my neglect. I have always regretted that I had measured his health using my own youthful standards.

Now that I was aware of neglecting my mother, I went to see Grandmaster to tell him that I wanted to go home. When I saw him in his study, I could not open my mouth to tell him this news because I was afraid he would be disappointed in my decision, for it meant discontinuing my Tai Chi studies. Finally I built up enough courage to say timidly, "Grandmaster, I want to go home and care for my mother."

"Good! Yee, you finally realize that you need to give love to your family instead of taking their love for granted." Grandmaster greeted my request with enthusiasm.

"Why is family so important, Grandmaster?" I asked.

"Family provides us with an opportunity to learn to live with one another harmoniously without always being fearful of making mistakes. In a family, we learn that people of different ages have different needs.

"Children need adult supervision just as sheep need shepherds. The road in front of them is full of choices. If not careful, the young could make the wrong choice and go astray easily." He went on to tell me a story, "Once there was a farmer who had lost one of his goats. He tried to find it by tracking it down along the only road leading from his house. When he reached a two-way junction, he asked his son to pursue one of them. When he reached a three-way junction, he summoned his neighbors for help. Finally they all came back empty-handed. His wife asked why they could not find the goat. 'My dear wife, when we reached the end of the road, there were more and more junctions,' replied the distraught farmer.

The bowl was extremely hot but I ignored it because I wanted my father to get well soon. When he took the bowl, he immediately put it down on the table as the bowl scorched him. He looked at me and asked me to show him my hands--they were as red as a hot iron.

"Yee, do you think the goat would have been lost if the farmer had supervised its journey?"

"Grandmaster, I think the goat should be safe under the guardianship of the farmer, even though it is still possible for the goat to get lost," I replied.

"I agree with you, Yee. Similarly, if an adult can supervise a child, the child will have a better chance to remain on his proper course to adulthood. Young people are in a period of growth and are eager to learn and imitate the behavior of the world around them. A concerned adult understands the importance of the environment for the development of a child. The mother of Meng Tsu, a famous scholar, a contemporary of Confucius, knew the needs of her child well. When she saw her son imitate an undertaker, she moved her family away from the adjacent funeral home. When she saw him imitate a carpenter, she moved her family away from the carpentry shop. Finally she settled down when she saw her son reading a book in imitation of the students in the neighborhood school. Eventually her son became one of the greatest scholars of all time."

"Now that I understood the needs of the young members of a family," I asked, "What can adults learn from each other in a family, Grandmaster?"

"Adults can learn to resolve conflict by love and understanding instead of by force. In a family, the siblings can learn to love each other despite quarrels. One time a notorious general was about to execute his flamboyant younger brother. Their mother intervened to no avail and left the house with a broken heart, leaving a pot of green beans still cooking in the kitchen unattended. When the general fed more straw to keep up the fire for the beans, his brother came up with a poem to plead for his life:

> 'Beans are cooked by the bean straw;
> Beans are weeping in the bean stew.
> Aren't we coming from the same family?
> Why are you frying me so earnestly?'

"The general sighed and changed his mind about executing his brother.

"Yee, if we can understand the needs of a family, we can understand the needs of our society. If we can understand the needs of our society, we can understand the needs of our world. Then people in the world can live harmoniously and in peace among themselves and among nations."

I nodded and asked further, "Grandmaster, what about the old? What are their needs?"

"Yee, do you remember this poem?

"Under the roof there were two swallows, flying happily one male and one female.

Mouthful of clay between beams, a family of four were born to the nest.

Four children grew day and night, fighting for food ceaselessly.

Green worms were hard to find, yellow mouths were never satisfied.

Mouths and claws were exhausted, only love could be oblivious to tiredness.

To and fro ten times in an instant, still afraid the nest is hungry.

Arduous work for thirty days, mother was thin and children were strong.

Patiently taught them to speak, carefully brushed their feathers.

Feathers were full, time to guide to the tree branches.

Flew, flew high and never turned their heads, dispersing like the wind into four directions.

Male and female were calling in the air, coarse sounds and no returns.

Came back to an empty nest, sorrowful through the night.

'Swallows, swallows, don't feel sad, you should recall your own acts.

Remember in your younger days, the time when you flew high and abandoned your mother?

The feelings of your parents then, you ought to know by now.'

"As you see, Yee, the poem is talking about us. Many of us fly away from our parents once we have reached adulthood and seldom look back at them. Even though we love our parents, we tend to take their needs for granted. Many a time we think that they are happy and comfortable in their 'empty nests.' But are they? When was the last time you saw your mother?"

When Grandmaster finished talking, I felt remorse because I realized I was no better than a swallow. I made up my mind to return to my mother when the first harbinger of spring made its appearance.

Then one day when I was preparing for my trip home, I heard some unusual noises down the road. At first I thought Grandmaster had come home early from the marketplace. But when I saw a body being carried into the house, I sensed that something terrible had happened. Rushing into the house, I found Lotus lying on her bed with blood dripping from her mouth; her hands were cold and lifeless and her face was as white as ashes. I held her bloodless hands and called her name repeatedly, trying desperately to revive her, but all efforts were in vain.

The doctor came and examined her, and asked what had happened. According to witnesses, Lotus was bitten by a strange animal in the field. The doctor opened her eyes and found the pupils to be dilated and spiritless. He looked at me and asked me to give him a white sheet; he covered her motionless body from head to toe with the sheet and left the room without saying a word. Overwhelmed by this sudden and unbearable grief, I fled the room and ran to the Reflecting Pond.

Sitting on the ground where I had spent so many precious hours with my dear Lotus, I touched the jade stone hanging from my neck. Memories of Lotus rushed back to me: I remembered the first outing we had when we went to the marketplace in a horse cart. We were sitting in the back seats while Grandmaster was in the front. Even though I was not looking at her, like a magnet, Lotus had drawn me closer and closer until our bodies touched. Both our hearts were beating rapidly. At that moment, the world seemed to have remained motionless as we two fused into one. Without words we seemed to have promised our lives to each other for eternity. We separated immediately when Grandmaster turned around in search of his hat.

The next morning Lotus gave me this jade necklace shaped like a tear, wrapped in a paper with a story and these words written on it: "If a man does not make an effort to study diligently while he is young and able, he will regret it in his old age when he no longer can." The story was about a young husband who abandoned his studies and returned to his beautiful wife from a faraway school. When he entered the house, he was surprised to see his wife cutting her unfinished silk cloth into half. "Why are you cutting up the silk cloth, my dear wife? Have you not almost finished weaving it?" asked the husband. "Yes, my dear husband, it has been halfway done, so have your studies," replied the wife. Her husband got the point and returned to school to finish his studies.

Even though we had had no more close bodily contact since that time, Lotus had given me the best of her love--being understanding and motivating me to move upward. Now my dear Lotus was gone and I missed her unceasingly. The sky is timeless and the earth is ageless, yet they will end some day; our love is so pure and true that it will never end.

Around the Reflecting Pond, everything seemed to remind me of Lotus, so I closed my eyes and tried to find comfort inside myself. In my mind, I heard a voice saying, "This too shall pass. This too shall pass."

"Yes," I replied, "it shall pass, but until then, it is cutting me like a knife." The voice was silent.

I opened my eyes and saw some ants on the ground busy gathering food. A thought flashed through my mind: If Lotus were in Heaven, why couldn't I join her? At the same instance, I heard a voice saying, "Even ants want to live."

"I hate ants!" I raised my leg to stomp on the tiny creatures. But just before my foot reached them, I heard the voice again, "Let them live, my child." I averted my killing foot and threw myself onto the ground. "Why? Even ants can live; spiders can live; birds can live; frogs can live; but my dearest Lotus cannot?" I finally broke down and cried like a child.

The voice continued, "Sometimes it is difficult to understand, my child, but miracles do happen, my child. Miracles do happen, my child."

After a while I heard a loud sound arising from the water. A huge frog was trying to jump toward rays of sunlight, which had penetrated the dark clouds and fallen onto the middle of the pond. As I wondered what the frog was trying to do, suddenly I remembered Great-Great-Grandmaster's goal. Maybe the frog is trying to jump out of this physical world into a spiritual world. Is there life after life?" Awed by the magnificent shaft of sunlight, I felt so insignificant and vulnerable. Humbly, I knelt down and prayed for our souls. Instead of decrying the seemingly inhuman nature of the tragedy, I thanked Heaven for the little I still had left in this world and begged for mercy. Having completely surrendered my pride, my ambition, and my future to Heaven, my mind had calmed down; I felt I was surrounded by the warmth of love as though someone were embracing me.

As I prayed, the image of the Reflecting Pond appeared in my mind. The water in the pond was turning tumultuously as if in a severe storm. Refusing to let the violent image of a storm tempt me to decry my fate again, I continued to pray fervently for mercy. When I absolutely relinquished my power to Heaven, the turbulence stopped and the pond became still. I meditated by focusing my mind on the water surface. After a while, I saw a few bubbles appear in the perfectly calm water. As more bubbles came up, I saw a beautiful red flower slowly emerge! The lovely flower opened gently, showing four magnificent crimson petals. It was the miracle ginseng flower which I had risked my life to fetch! I jumped up instantly and dashed into the underground storage room.

I found the flower still in the jar, as fresh as if it had been picked yesterday. I took it out and boiled it in a porcelain pot to extract its ingredients as herbal medicine. When the medicine was ready, I carried it to Lotus and carefully fed her the miracle herb. As the herb reached her lips, her tongue, and finally her heart, Lotus gradually regained her color and her hands became warm again!

"She's alive! She's alive!" I could not contain my excitement. Looking to the sky through the window, I nodded and smiled.

Lotus woke up, held my hands and said, "Yee, I had a dream."

"What was your dream, Lotus?"

"I dreamed I was flying toward a beautiful rainbow."

"Were you afraid?"

"No, I felt at peace. I felt myself gently moving onward when I heard a voice. Someone was calling my name. At first I ignored the call, but finally, as the calls became more earnest, I turned my head from the rainbow and I saw you. That was when I awoke."

"I must have had a gigantic voice," I teased her, and told her about the miracle flower.

"Where is Grandpa?"

"I am here, my child." Grandmaster had just arrived after being informed of his grandchild's illness by someone in the marketplace. Grandmaster held her hands for a long time without speaking, as if he were meditating.

Next morning I talked to Grandmaster at the Reflecting Pond. "Grandmaster, were you praying or meditating while you were holding Lotus's hands yesterday?"

"Yee, I was praying."

"Why do people always want to pray?"

"Why does water always want to go downward?" Grandmaster replied, adding "Even people with 'iron' hearts will cry for mercy in moments of crises."

"Then is it natural for people to believe in Heaven and prayers?"

"Ask your own heart, Yee."

I asked my heart and became confused--one side of me wanted to believe in Heaven because prayers had given me peace; yet another side of me refused to believe because I could not see or touch Heaven like one sees or touches a person.

Bewildered, I asked, "Grandmaster, is it possible that someone believes in Heaven and at the same time he doubts its very existence?"

Grandmaster answered, "Yes, even the most religious person in the world will sometimes doubt the existence of Heaven when misfortune befalls innocent people; yet his doubts will not shake his belief in Heaven."

"How do you know, Grandmaster?"

"Yee, I am not a teacher of religion but I do know that people have yin and yang minds. The yin mind accepts Heaven readily while the yang mind doubts its existence because it won't easily accept anything it cannot actually experience. As human beings, we will always have doubts. After all, isn't it Heaven that gives us both minds? Therefore, it would be fruitless to fight against these doubts. If you follow the force of nature, you will love your humanity instead of hating it for doubting your own faith. But remember: Although we have doubts, we will always have faith. This is also natural, and so follow your own heart and pray."

"What do you pray for, Grandmaster?"

"Health, wealth, and happiness. In fact, I pray every day."

"Grandmaster, if we pray automatically in moment of crises, why do we make efforts to pray every day?"

"Yee, remember the old saying 'What you think during the day is what you will dream of at night'? Our mind works on the things we pray about even in our dreams. Besides, I believe that the essences of the things we pray for do exist in this world and they are connected in some way. Therefore, each time we pray, we are opening up channels in ourselves to these wonderful things and we attract them to our way. The things we pray for sincerely have a better chance to become a reality; at the least we will have a peaceful feeling after prayers. So follow your heart and pray."

I thanked Grandmaster for his lesson and he left the Reflecting Pond. Facing the quiet water alone, I contemplated Grandmaster's teachings on family: Why is it easier to judge the needs of other members of my family by using my own standards? Is it because I already know my needs, hence it is easier to project them onto other family members than to make an effort to understand their needs? Are family members important to me? If so, shouldn't I put aside my point of view and make an effort to understand how they view the world? If I can do that, do I still worry about what life has in store for me? Isn't love, happiness and harmony in a family what I yearn for?

Then I turned my thoughts to Grandmaster's teachings regarding prayers. What did he mean when he said he prayed for health, wealth, and happiness every day? Yes, it is true that Tai Chi movements have kept our bodies healthy. But again could it have prevented the wild animal from biting Lotus? If we do not totally control our own health, who does?

My mind then turned to the meaning of wealth. Why do I want to pray for wealth? Do I want to become the man who once stole a pot of gold and when the judge asked why he had done it, he answered because he had seen only the pot of gold, not the people nearby? Or do I want to become the man who was swimming across a river with a sack of gold; when he could not go on, his companion suggested that he abandon his gold, but he refused and finally sank into the riverbed with his sack of gold? No, I don't want either. I just want to have enough riches to provide for my family and to keep me from worrying about where my next meal is coming from. I want the freedom to do what I like to do, not to do what I have to. But who decides who has and who has not?

Why do I pray for happiness? When I have both health and wealth, happiness would then be easy to obtain. But when I have none, what then? Who will give me the strength to keep on smiling every day? Who can uplift my spirits to the end?

Then I contemplated in terms of yin and yang about the world we are living in: Maybe there is a spiritual, yin world where there is hope and justice for all and to it we can pray for our peace of mind. On the other hand, maybe we could love each other starting with our own family in this physical, yang world so that with love, we could all live in peace and harmony among our neighbors, societies, and nations.

When I realized that the yin and yang worlds could exist in harmony, I felt as if a soft light had entered my body from above and had expanded inside my body to radiate outward, encompassing my whole being. At that moment I felt totally and completely imbued with love and peace. A joyful smile sparkled in my eyes because I had been blessed with the Seventh Secret of the Tai Chi Circle. These words echoed through my soul:

Love and understand my family now, for harmony starts where the hearth is; humbly pray for health, wealth, happiness, and all the precious things life has to offer.

Love and understand my family now, for harmony starts where the hearth is; humbly pray for health, wealth, happiness, and all the precious things life has to offer.

Love and understand my family now, for harmony starts where the hearth is; humbly pray for health, wealth, happiness, and all the precious things life has to offer.

Chapter Nine

Butterflies

One morning as I walked by Grandmaster's study I heard him laughing heartily. I went inside and found him alone, laughing.

"Good morning, Yee," Grandmaster greeted me with some laughter still visible on his countenance. "Please join me for breakfast."

There were some boiled eggs and baked yams on the table. Before I could ask why he had been laughing, Grandmaster addressed me, "Please, sit down and have something to eat."

I sat and picked up a yam. He commented, "Laughter, like yams, is good for you. It can uplift your spirits and lighten your load."

"Grandmaster, I agree that yams and laughter are both good for us, but there is a big difference between them: We can have yams whenever we want them, but that is not the case with laughter."

"Yee, can you tell me why we can have yams whenever we want them?"

"Because we have learned from our ancestors how to plant the yams, protect the seedlings from insects, fertilize the plants, harvest the yams, and store them for later use."

"What would have happened if nobody had taught us how to plant yams?"

"The yams would have grown in the wild."

"Do you think we could then have had yams whenever we wanted them?"

"No, Grandmaster, the supply of yams would have depended on the whims of the weather, the absence of insects, and the lack of weeds."

"Likewise the supply of laughter would depend on the mood of the person, the absence of hostility, and the nature of the humor?" Grandmaster made his point.

"Do you mean laughter can be cultivated?"

"Yes."

"How?"

"It is simple. Every day as soon as you wake up, choose a place, go there, and start laughing. Remember to make use of your mind, Yee? You can persuade your mind to believe whatever you wish it to. You can laugh by deliberately remembering some humorous pictures and recalling them each morning."

"How can I laugh if I don't feel like laughing?"

"You must force yourself to open your mouth and flash your teeth and repeat this maneuver a number of times. Once you have overcome your reluctance, you will be able to laugh easily."

After saying that, Grandmaster stood up and told me to follow him to the Reflecting Pond for my lesson. I sensed something important was about to happen. When we arrived at a flat grassy area next to the pond, Grandmaster told me that he was going to test my Tai Chi skills. So he asked me to form a Horse Stance.

"Are you ready, Yee?"

"Yes, Grandmaster," I replied confidently because like the Putee Tree, I had rooted myself securely into the ground.

Grandmaster applied forces on my body from different directions, but I was able to deal with them and remained in perfect balance. Like a pine tree following the wind, I followed his forces smoothly without the slightest awkwardness. Suddenly, Grandmaster drew an extremely light circle on my chest with his index finger, intending to distract my attention and thus giving him a chance to uproot me; but I was able to sense even these delicate forces and accordingly relaxed my chest, leaving no opportunity for Grandmaster to achieve his purpose.

"Good! You've mastered it. You've mastered it!" Grandmaster repeatedly praised me. Knowing that words were also a means to lure me into losing my balance, I kept my emotions in check and was not overjoyed. Suddenly without warning, Grandmaster swept my leg with his No Shadow Leg from underneath. The instant that I felt his leg touch mine, I shifted my body weight to the other leg, forming a Golden Cock Single Stance posture, and thus keeping my body in perfect balance. "Good!" Grandmaster exclaimed and nodded contentedly. Then he told me he was going to test my Push Hands skills.

In Push Hands exercise, it is almost an unspoken rule that at the very beginning one starts to meet the right hand of his opponent with his own right hand. However, in this case, Grandmaster unexpectedly raised his left hand instead of the customary right hand and instantly attacked me from the very beginning. Luckily I had been trained to expect the unexpected and I was able to neutralize his attack by making a circle. Abandoning his left hand, Grandmaster advanced with his right hand in a "curve seeking straight" manner toward the vital point in my shoulder. Sensing his movement, I turned slightly to the left, rendering his attack ineffective.

Grandmaster's body was now exposed for attack when his fist had failed to land on my body. I immediately took advantage of this opening and used the Grasp Sparrow's Tail technique to attack him. When my hand reached for his body, Grandmaster raised his right hand in a circular motion to meet my arm halfway. Even though the touch of his hand was extremely light, I immediately sensed I was losing my balance. This ability to maintain one's sensibilities even during high speed sparring was the result of years of training in slow movements. As soon as I noted that my balance was affected, I halted my attack, thus avoiding the same fate as that of the bully master four years ago when Grandmaster used the same movement to toss him.

When I retreated, Grandmaster advanced with a High Pat on Horse movement toward my head. I warded off his attack using a White Crane Spreading Wings maneuver. Our bodies remained perfectly relaxed through all this action. Only with a completely relaxed body could one sense the slightest movement of his opponent and react automatically to any sudden attack. Grandmaster raised his leg so lightly and quickly that it would have been almost impossible to defend myself if I had not already developed a reflex reaction to deal with it. I dropped my hand on his knee naturally, forcing him to retreat. "Excellent!" exclaimed Grandmaster.

Grandmaster had tested every aspect of my skills. He now stepped into the open and said solemnly, "Yee, attack me as if you were in a life and death situation." It sounded like a genuine order and, to show my respect, I needed to obey. I knew that our fight would not be an endless one in which we hurt each other needlessly, because in a high level fight a winner can be distinguished immediately, even after a single engagement. By now I also understood that if I had too strong a desire to win, I would defeat myself even before I started. So I prepared myself to accept any possible outcome of the fight. My mind remained as calm as still water; I neither had a desire to win nor a desire to lose.

It was high noon and the sun was directly above us. There was no wind and everything seemed to be standing still as Grandmaster tested my learning. The Reflecting Pond was calm; it too, seemed to be holding its breath, watching my performance.

Grandmaster stood firmly on the ground and appeared as calm as the distant mountains. His eyes sparkled with vitality, and his movements were steady and sure; only his gray hair gave away his advanced age. My body radiated with energy and my movements were quick and nimble, but the uncertainty in my eyes gave away my youth and inexperience. So two human beings, one old and one young, both perfect in their own right, circled each other in fighting positions, forgetting for a moment that they were teacher and student, but true followers of the immortal Tai Chi Chuan.

We both understood that whoever lost his concentration first would lose; and if both were at their highest level of concentration, the one who moved first would lose. So we faced each other for a long time without either of us making any advances. A thought flashed through my mind: Perhaps I could use my advantage as a youth to outlast Grandmaster, who should be getting tired very soon. So the moment I saw him change his front leg position, apparently to give it a rest, I lunged forward. Grandmaster immediately perceived my intention and trapped my hand with his. Feeling I was losing my balance, I instantly made a circle to stabilize myself, and retreated at the same time. During our normal practice sessions, Grandmaster would ordinarily stop at this point, and we would then start again. However, this was not a normal practice or a normal time. Like a Dragon Whirl Typhoon in the shape of an inverted funnel, Grandmaster tightened his grip by making smaller and smaller circles while I neutralized them with even smaller circles, all happening at the speed of thought. In a flash, Grandmaster reduced the attacking circle to a point, which was beyond my ability to neutralize. Like a Dragon Whirl Typhoon, which had touched down on the ground, I was being swept high into the sky.

Still in the sky, I glimpsed Grandmaster: Like a proud grandfather throwing his grandchild into the air, he seemed to be very joyful. I, too, seemed to enjoy being thrown, yet instead of falling back into his loving hands, *splash!* into the Reflecting Pond I went! I swam back to shore, realizing that I had a lot to learn from him.

When I got out of the water, Grandmaster held my hands and said, "Yee, I have taught you everything I know. From now on you are free to go." I was surprised to know that I had just finished my last Tai Chi lesson.

"Grandmaster, I still have so much to learn from you."

"Yee, Tai Chi is a way of life and I can only do so much for you, the rest will depend on you to discover. Tai Chi is an exercise of mind over body. You have already developed the ability to relax your body, even when under attack. This ability has eluded many of my students because it is natural for people to resist force with force. Indeed you are the best student I have ever had."

"But, Grandmaster, you still can toss me wherever you want to. How can I come to be as good as you if you are not going to teach me any more?" I asked, thinking Grandmaster might change his mind.

"My family has made a solemn promise to yours that we would teach you everything we know, and I have done so. I have not kept any secrets from you, Yee," Grandmaster told me sincerely.

"Grandmaster, you obviously know things I don't know. Is it because of my age?"

"Yee, it has nothing to do with your age. It is your mind. You have reached the stage of letting go of your body. The next stage you need to reach is to let go of your mind as well."

"Grandmaster, how can I let go of my mind if the art of Tai Chi is all about the mind?"

"In order to gain, you must lose first. You will obtain enlightenment one day if you keep the secrets of the Tai Chi Circle in mind. Only then can you make circles as small as a point and surpass me in the martial art of Tai Chi. But remember, the true purpose of Tai Chi is to obtain life, not the power to destroy it."

Then I remembered his goal picture showing the small bird on a tiny leaf and asked, "Grandmaster, can you explain the meaning of the poem written on your picture of the meditating bird? I still don't understand it."

"Yee, you need to experience it because no words can explain it. If you have faith in the Tai Chi Circle and live by its principles, you will understand this one day, only then can you return to nature." Grandmaster left, and I was alone.

As I stood there, I recalled my first Tai Chi lesson and the countless hours I had spent under this Putee Tree since then. Throughout the years, I had stretched my body's tolerance to its limit and finally, just like the Putee Tree, I was able to root myself into the ground.

I looked at the Reflecting Pond and remembered how many times it had reflected its wisdom to me. Indeed it was like my own mirror in which I had clearly seen my true self at times when my thoughts were clouded.

These words, which had inspired me, still were ingrained vividly in my mind:

Putee Tree is my root;

Reflecting Pond is my mirror.

Sweep my body and mind daily I must,

To keep them away from the worldly dust.

Since Grandmaster had spoken about returning to nature, I looked around, and finding nobody watching, I stripped myself of my wet clothes and was now naked in this wilderness. Inhaling deeply, I filled myself with the fragrance of the wildflowers; exhaling slowly and evenly, I rooted myself to the ground and started to practice the Tai Chi movements one more time under the Putee Tree. My hands and legs were tensionless, and I felt my body moving effortlessly as though I were moving in water.

As I progressed in the form, my body became so light that I felt as if I were rooting into the ground without touching it, while my body was buoyed up by water. Every hair of my body seemed to be suspended in it.

As I progressed further into the form, I developed some strange feelings for the very first time. My body became so insubstantial that I felt as if I were moving on water! I could now direct my body anywhere I wished without experiencing the slightest resistance. I had lost all consciousness of time and space. Tai Chi and I had become one.

I forgot how long I was doing my Tai Chi form before I saw something moving in front of me. Drawing nearer, I saw it was a beautiful butterfly stretching its wings and legs, as if it were just getting up from a deep sleep.

Strangely I seemed to have become the butterfly myself. I woke up, flapping my wings as though I were startled and exclaimed, "What a dream I had! I dreamed I had become human! Am I still in a dream or not?" I flapped my wings gently and glided by a few flowers. I did one of my favorite tricks--diving vertically downward and coming straight up just before striking the ground. I am not in a dream, I assured myself.

It was a beautiful day as I flapped along through the air, visiting flower after flower. Passing over the Reflecting Pond, I dove toward it until I almost hit the water and for an instant I glimpsed my image. When I came up into the air the image registered in my mind. Was that my image? Impossible! It was a healthy human child with rosy cheeks. It was the same human I had dreamed of before, but much younger. Am I in a dream again? Having heard that a dreamer has no sense of taste, I flew immediately to my usual place, went straight to the heart of the biggest flower and drank its nectar. It was sweet! I was not in a dream!

So I forgot about dreaming and continued to enjoy life as usual as I swooped through flowery bushes, cavorting with other butterflies. The sky had turned red and I knew the sun would soon be gone, so I decided to go home before dark. As I was returning to my home in the Putee Tree, I flew over the Reflecting Pond again. In a playful mood I dove vertically down toward the pond and then shot straight upward. But I was stunned when I glimpsed my image as that of an old man with gray hair. Can the same person have grown so much in such a short time? Am I in a dream again? But I was too tired to attempt to prove to myself that I was a butterfly and not human. Reaching my home, I closed my wings and went to sleep.

I drew my hands inward and straightened my legs as I finished my Tai Chi movements. Immediately, I dashed to the pond and looked at my reflection. There was neither butterfly nor gray hair! I put some water in my mouth and tasted it. It was refreshing. I raised my hands and shouted, "I am not in a dream!"

When I calmed down, I asked myself once more, "Or am I? Am I the dream of the butterfly? Or do I dream of the butterfly? But what is the difference?" I stared at the water for a long time, trying to understand what I had just experienced. Indeed, life is so short that it would pass in the blink of an eye. When I looked back at the days I had lived, my past appeared just like a dream. After a while, I recalled these lines from Grandmaster's painting:

Indeed the Putee Tree has no root.

Also the Reflecting Pond has no mirror;

My body and mind are nothing but emptiness.

Tell me then, where do I get the worldly dust to sweep?

If I am but an emptiness, what would be the meaning of my life? As I was considering the meaning of life, I began once more to practice my Tai Chi movements. Soon I reached a high degree of meditation through my movements. My body had become so light that when a weightless feather fell on my arm, it caused my arm to sink; and when a fly tried to land on my hand, it too, failed to find solid ground and fell off.

As my state of meditation became deeper and deeper, I lost consciousness of space and time. Suddenly, I saw someone coming toward me from the other side of the Reflecting Pond, riding on a bamboo branch! When he reached the shore, I realized it was Lao Tsu, the famous Taoist. I took this opportunity to ask, "Sir, what is the meaning of life?"

"The Tao begot one. One begot two. Two begot three. And the three begot the ten thousand things. The ten thousand things carry yin and embrace yang."

Am I the dream of the butterfly? Or do I dream of the butterfly?
But what is the difference?" ... Indeed, life is so short that it would
pass in the blink of an eye. When I looked back at the days I had
lived, my past appeared just like a dream.

127

"What do you mean, sir?"

"The Tao is nature. The universe started from one point, which expanded into yin and yang; yin and yang gave birth to a third, and so on. To understand nature, one needs to go back from ten thousand things to three, from three to two, and from two to one. To find oneself, one goes back to nature through the same route," Lao Tsu answered.

"I still don't understand it, sir." His wisdom remained a mystery to me.

"Tao that can be explained is not real Tao. In my book *Tao Te Ching* I have used the word 'baby' many times, trying to capture some aspects of Tao. Let me use the example of a baby to give you a glimpse of Tao. Before a baby is born, he is one. After he is born, his world becomes two, simple yin and yang--hungry and not hungry, crying and not crying, light and no light. As he continues to grow his world becomes three as life becomes more complicated when yin and yang intertwine with each other. For example, when he is still young, his mother punishes him by slapping his face--the action indicates hatred, yet it contains love, yin within yang. As he matures, he interacts with many people and things, resulting in ten thousand emotional combinations. The countless interactions are still made up of the basic elements yin and yang. So in order to return to Tao, one should look beyond the every day complexities of things into its very heart, its yin and yang."

"So the world of a baby is simple yet it is closer to Tao and, since Tao is nature, we should return to being a baby in order to be closer to nature?" I asked.

"Yes, as a baby you are free from the endless emotional burdens which accumulate with age. Being a baby you have nothing to lose. You have not yet tasted life so you are not afraid to lose it; you have not attached yourself to anyone so you are free of obligations; you have no earthly possessions so you are not obsessed by them; you have no ambition so you are not haunted by your failures; and you are merely a blank paper without meaning so you are free from asking the meaning of life." After answering my questions, Lao Tsu hopped back onto his bamboo branch and sailed away across the Reflecting Pond.

I woke up from my meditation as I finished my Tai Chi movements. Facing the Reflecting Pond, I felt a lust for life like that of a baby had returned to me. Feeling eternal youth, I ran toward the pond and raised my hands high with cries of joy, "I am a baby! I am young forever! I will live forever! What has a baby got to lose? I know that with every action I take, I will gain one more life experience. The more I act, the more I will gain. Why should I wait until tomorrow to do what I can do today? I will do it now so that I can go on to experience new and exciting things in this wonderful world! I do it now! I do it now! I do it now! Why should I wait passively for life to come by? From now on, I will go for the joy of life! The joy of life! The joy of life!"

While acting like a child, full of zest for life, I suddenly discovered I was also behaving like an old man, laughing heartily at myself and the world, saying "All things shall come to pass. This, too, could be my last shining moment in this world. Since my life could end tomorrow, why should I take myself so seriously? Laugh at my failures! Laugh at my worries! Laugh at my successes! Laugh at my fate! If life will go on as usual after I am gone, then why should I take the world so seriously? From now on, I will laugh at the world! I laugh at the world! I laugh at the world!"

I realized that within myself, yin and yang were coexisting in harmony, forming a powerful life-force. Indeed, I had been transformed into a Tai Chi Circle in which my yang half was acting as if my life could go on forever and my yin half was behaving as if this moment was my last. As soon as I realized I had been enlightened with the Eighth Secret of the Tai Chi Circle, I felt warmth inside. When I closed my eyes, I saw a beautiful Tai Chi Circle glowing half in gold and half in red in my mind. Then the colors entered separately into each of my eyes, vitalizing them with energy. When I opened my eyes again, I saw a different world--water just being formless by itself and flowers just being red themselves. When I looked at myself, I saw myself just being myself--a precious living creature playing a role in the hierarchy of things in this moment of time. Indeed, I perceived things in their real nature and no longer projected my own judgment on them. With much joy, I understood that I, too, had finally become an enlightened Tai Chi master.

With no family oath to keep, I was free to share the secrets of the Tai Chi Circle with the world. I was ready to travel home and then to the world. I put on my clothes, which had dried in the sun, and went to see my dear Lotus.

"Lotus, I am leaving tomorrow, and I have come to say goodbye to you until we see each other again," I told her when I found her near the mountain stream.

"Are you leaving me behind?" she was surprised.

"The journey will be difficult. Besides, I want to establish myself in the outside world before I come back for you."

"Yee, near or far, I will follow you wherever you go. I'm yours--unless you don't want me." Lotus ran quickly back toward the house.

I ran after her and held her hands, "Lotus, I love you. I fell in love with you the very first time I saw you. We have gone through joys and sorrows together. We have bonded to each other through life and death. Lotus, you are the only woman I will ever want. I will love you forever." I kissed her for the first time. I felt wonderful, for I was about to take an important step in my life.

"Lotus, please wait. I am going to see Grandmaster. We need his blessings." I ran to Grandmaster's study and found him writing at his desk. I shouted excitedly, "Grandmaster!" He turned around and our eyes met, penetrating each other's soul like true Tai Chi masters. He gave me an understanding smile for he understood that I, too, had obtained the Tai Chi Circle enlightenment.

"I can see you have good news for me, Yee," Grandmaster greeted me.

"Yes, Grandmaster. Indeed, I have another piece of good news."

"Double Happiness! What is the other piece of good news?"

"With your permission, I want to marry your granddaughter, Lotus."

Grandmaster did not answer but turned around and looked at the Tai Chi Circle. Not sure how he was reacting to my request, I pleaded, "Please, Grandmaster. I love your granddaughter very much and I will take good care of her."

"I know you will, Grandson," Grandmaster replied happily as he turned to face me. "After eight hundred years our two families have finally completed the Tai Chi Circle. We have become one."

So with Grandmaster's blessings, Lotus and I bade Grandmaster and others goodbye as we planned to leave very early in the morning.

Next day before dawn, we mounted our horses and left the village without disturbing anyone. When we reached the mountainside I saw someone waiting. I pushed forward on my horse and when I reached the figure, I recognized that it was Grandmaster.

"Yee, I've come here to say goodbye."

Emotion overcame me and I knelt down before my Grandmaster, "Grandpa, thank you for your teachings. I will not disgrace our family names."

"I know you won't, Grandson. You have never walked away from honor since the very first time I met you." Grandmaster handed me the Tai Chi Circle. "Take this jade plate with you. It will protect you on your journey."

I received the precious plate and bowed to my Grandmaster. The sun had just risen in the horizon and our surroundings bustled with life once more. Remembering that Grandmaster had given me my student name, I turned around and asked a last question, "Grandpa, what is the meaning of my name?"

"Yee means the mind. Tai Chi is all about your mind. Remember my grandson, it is all in your mind." Grandmaster waved his hand as our horses galloped down the mountain.

Like two beautiful butterflies in springtime, Lotus and I flew happily toward our destinies. As I was embarking on my new journey in life, these words lingered in my mind:

Laugh at the world, for it is all in my mind; now it is up to me to paint the color of my life.

Laugh at the world, for it is all in my mind; now it is up to me to paint the color of my life.

Laugh at the world, for it is all in my mind; now it is up to me to paint the color of my life.

101 Lessons

of

TAO

Inner Harmony • Self-Awareness • Wellness

Luke Chan

Author of *Secrets of the Tai Chi Circle: Journey to Enlightenment*

Seriously-Humorous Anecdotes
helping you discover how
to live life to its fullest.

101 Lessons of Tao

These ancient stories of Tao will cause you to both laugh and learn. Reading each story is like looking into a still pond, with one aspect of your life reflected back to you. By recognizing the yings and yangs of your life, you can achieve a balanced state of Tao for optimal living. By knowing that others share your behavior, you can prevent yourself from feeling isolated and taking things too personally, thereby increasing your self-esteem and morale.

Truly inspirational stories of 101 individuals who miraculously recovered from cancer, diabetes, arthritis, paralysis, heart disease, severe depression, systemic lupus, and many other chronic illnesses.

Learn the self-healing method prescribed by the world's largest medicineless hospital for curing the incurables.

Discover the exercise practiced daily by eight million people for health, longevity, creativity, and mental clarity.

Luke Chan

101 Miracles of Natural Healing (book and videotape)

Features truly inspirational stories of 101 individuals who miraculously recovered from cancer, diabetes, arthritis, heart disease, severe depression, paralysis, systemic lupus, and many other chronic illnesses. This book also shows you how to do the self-healing exercise used by those individuals to achieve health, longevity, creativity and mental clarity.

ORDER FORM

Title	Price	Qty	Amount
Chi-Lel™ Qigong News			
Subscription (4 issues per year).....	$ 15.00	_____	_____
101 Miracles of Natural Healing			
Book	$ 14.95	_____	_____
Videotape	$ 24.95	_____	_____
Audiotapes:			
First 100-day Gong	$ 10.00	_____	_____
Second 100-day Gong	$ 10.00	_____	_____
Third 100-day Gong	$ 10.00	_____	_____
Fourth 100-day Gong	$ 10.00	_____	_____
Secrets of the Tai Chi Circle: Journey to Enlightenment			
Book	$ 10.00	_____	_____
Audiotape (unabridged recording, 4 tapes)	$ 24.95	_____	_____
101 Lessons of Tao			
Book	$ 12.95	_____	_____

($4.00 for first item, $.50 each additional item)

Postage and Handling: $_____

Ohio residents add 6% sales tax.   **Sales Tax: $**_____

Total Amount Due: $_____

To order, please complete this form and send with check or money order to:
Benefactor Press, 9676 Cinti-Columbus Road, Cincinnati, OH 45241

Name _____ Telephone ( ) _____

Address _____

City _____ State _____ Zip _____

Visa or Master Card Orders: 1-800-784-0146

Please allow 1-2 weeks for delivery

...the sun just coming up...birds, insects, animals, grass, bushes, trees, all seemed to know that they, too, are one day younger than tomorrow and joined in to celebrate today.